MOUNTAIN BIKE GUIDE

Inverness, the Great Glen
& the Cairngorms

by

TIMOTHY KING &
DEREK PURDY

THE ERNEST PRESS

First published by The Ernest Press 1995
Second, revised edition 2004
© Copyright Timothy King & Derek Purdy

ISBN 0 948153 73 3

British Library Cataloguing-in-Publication Data has been registered with the British Library in Wetherby and is available on request.

Typeset by Stanningley Serif
Printed in China through Colorcraft Ltd., HK

Disclaimer:

Whilst we have made every effort to achieve accuracy in the production of material for use in this guide book, the author, publishers and copyright owners can take no responsibility for: trespass, irresponsible riding, any loss or damage to persons or property suffered as a result of the route descriptions or advice offered in this book.

The inclusion of a route in this guide does not guarantee that the path/track will remain a right of way. If conflict with landowners occurs, please be polite and leave by the shortest available route, then check the situation with the relevant authority.

It is worthwhile to emphasise that riders should give way to both pedestrians and horse riders, and should make every effort to warn others of their presence.

Recommended reading to check access: 'Heading for the Scottish Hills', published by the Scottish Mountaineering Trust, 2004,

Acknowledgements:

Timothy King hanks Susan Price for providing the excellent line drawings and for her support of this whole project.

Derek Purdy has checked and revised all the routes in the 1995 guide and added nine more. He thanks Jane Pringle, Ronnie Henderson, Andy Wells and Neil Welsh for their help.

CONTENTS

INTRODUCTION

This Guide provides detailed descriptions and illustration of 30 Mountain Bike routes in the Great Glen, The Cairngorms and Eastern Highlands of Northern Scotland. This area, extending from Ullapool in the north west to Fort William in the south and Tomintoul in the east, provides arguably one of the most varied, exciting and scenic mountain biking areas in Britain. Within it the off-road cyclist can enjoy unparalleled access to the countryside on hundreds of miles of off-road tracks and quiet unclassified roads.

The routes described in this Guide cover the broad range of scenery and topography that the area offers. The routes extend from the shores of the Dornoch and Moray Firth's, through farmland, woodland, and forests, along river valleys, across open moorland, around numerous lochs and among the spectacular heights of some of Britain's highest mountains.

The variety in the routes described make this guide a suitable companion for both the committed off-road cyclist and the Mountain Bike first timer. It also insures that whatever the season and whatever the weather there is a route that can be followed in safety.

There are numerous Mountain Bike Hire shops across the region and the location of some of these is noted in the text. When out of the saddle the region offers excellent tourist facilities, generous hospitality and a wide range of accommodation and other attractions.

Of the 30 routes described in this Guide, 24 are true off-road rides that require a suitable mountain bike. The other 6 routes make use of the excellent minor metalled roads that criss cross the area providing a speedier though safe and largely deserted cycling surface for any type of bicycle. These narrow lanes penetrate into some of the more remote areas of the region and provide an easier terrain for a more relaxing trip. They also provide an alternative for those days on which the weather precludes any serious ventures off road.

Each route description includes details of both road and rail access, of the facilities available in the immediate area and of some of the local places of interest.

RIGHTS OF ACCESS

It is often stated that there is no law of trespass in Scotland. This is incorrect. Scots law does however differ from that in England and Wales. In Scotland the act of trespass does not by itself give the landowner the right to bring a legal action against the trespasser. The landowner can only bring a legal case if he has suffered some physical damage to his land. The trespasser is still, however, under an obligation to leave the land if he is asked to do so.

Although Northern Scotland has perhaps the most extensive network of proper off-road tracks anywhere in Britain, only a relatively small number of these are defined as legal Rights of Way. The vast majority of these ancient drovers routes and military roads either do not connect public places and therefore fall outside the definition of a Right of Way, or have fallen into disuse and any Right of Way that may have existed has lapsed.

This does not mean that these tracks are necessarily off limits to the mountain biker. There exists in Scotland a long tradition of tolerance on the part of landowners who do allow people access across their land so that all can enjoy the countryside and the hills. It is this tolerance, which often extends in to open encouragement, that has generated the image of Scotland as a place where there is a total freedom to roam.

In the vast majority of cases, Estates and other landowners in Scotland are happy to see off-road cyclists using defined routes across their land. This amiable state of affairs is likely to continue as long as cyclists observe the simple rules of the countryside and the basic courtesies.

The routes described in this Guide have been limited to those tracks where either a clear Right of Way exists or where the owner of the land actively encourages use by off-road cyclists. This constraint has inevitably meant that many of the most challenging mountain top routes that the area has to offer have not been included. This does not mean, however, that this guide and its routes will not satisfy the most demanding of mountain bikers and provide an excellent introduction to the excellent off-road cycling that the Region offers.

Finally, it should be noted that there are some areas of the Scottish countryside that are of particular ecological sensitivity and these are places where off-road cyclists should not attempt to go. One of these areas is the top of the Cairngorm plateau.

GRADING SYSTEM

The grading system that has been used is unique but not infallible! It identifies the four basic individual elements of any cycle route; the type of cycling surface, the number and extent of the ascents, the general topographical conditions that will be experienced and the length of the route. These elements in combination provide an overall assessment of the physical effort involved in completing a route and the general nature of the terrain to be covered. Each of these individual elements has been broken down in to several different levels and each of these has been given a description and a corresponding score.

Element	Description	Score
Surface	Metalled road	1
	Forest road	2
	Four-wheel drive track	3
	Firm path	4
	Mud or grass	5
Ascent	Flat	1
	Gentle, short climbs	2

	Gentle, longer climbs	3
	Medium, short climbs	4
	Medium, longer climbs	5
	Energetic, short climbs	6
	Energetic, long climbs	7
General conditions	Low level, sheltered	1
	Low level, exposed	2
	Mid level, sheltered	3
	Mid level, exposed	4
	High level	5
Length	Up to 10 miles	1
	11 - 20 miles	2
	Over 20 miles	3

The total obtained from adding the individual scores has been classified according to the following system :

Total score	Route Designation
1 - 5	Easy
6 - 10	Moderate
11 - 15	Energetic
16 - 20	Strenuous

In attributing an individual score to each element of a route there is inevitably a degree of subjectivity involved. This is especially so in assessing the type of ascents that the route involves. However, it is hoped that some measure of objectivity has been included and that the overall scores and Route Designations do provide a useful guide to the general nature of each ride and that the component scores will provide an accurate assessment of what to expect.

MAPS

The map that accompanies each route description is provided as a general guide only and should not be relied upon. Each map is only a sketch but all have a small indicator of scale. No serious off-road cycling should be attempted without an Ordnance Survey map. The relevant Landranger Series 1 : 50 000 Sheet for each route is listed in the introductory note. An attempt has been made to describe at least two routes on each Landranger Sheet and where possible this has been extended to 3 or 4 Routes which involve a variety of different route designations. Five of the routes will also be found on the Ordnance Survey's larger 1 : 25 000 scale Outdoor Leisure Map Number 3.

EQUIPMENT

Off-road cycling does not require vast amounts of specialist gear but it is foolhardy to set out without the basics of a small tool and puncture repair kit, a pump, adequate warm clothing including wet weather gear, a whistle, a map, a survival bag – small, light and costing just a few pounds, it could save your life – a water bottle, emergency rations and a HELMET. Route descriptions are written on the assumption that a compass is carried, as is some means of calculating distance.

THE MOUNTAIN BIKE OFF ROAD CODE
Issued by the Mountain Bike Club

Only ride where you know you have a legal right
Always yield to horses and pedestrians
Avoid animals and crops. If this is not possible, keep contact to a minimum
Take all litter with you
Leave all gates as found

Keep the noise down
Do not get annoyed with anyone, it never solves any problems
Always try to be self sufficient for you and your bike
Never create a fire hazard

THE COUNTRY CODE
Issued by the Countryside Commission

Guard against the risk of fire
Fasten all gates
Keep dogs under proper control
Keep to paths
Avoid damaging fences, hedges and walls
Leave no litter
Safeguard water supplies
Protect wildlife, wild plants and trees
Go carefully on country roads
Respect the life of the countryside.

THE FOREST CODE
Issued by the Forest Authority

Guard against all risks of fire
Protect trees, plants and wildlife
Leave things as you find them, take nothing away
Keep dogs under proper control
Avoid damaging buildings, fences, hedges, walls and signs
Leave no litter
Respect the work of the forest
Observe signs, do not leave open or obstruct gates and for your own
safety keep clear of forestry operations
Finally respect the peace & quiet of the forest; avoid disturbing others.

THE FOREST CYCLING CODE
Issued by Forest Enterprise

Expect the unexpected. Keep your speed down.
Remember other vehicles use forest roads as well.
Give way to walkers - be friendly to other forest users.
Hail a horse and avoid an accident.
Danger! Keep away from all forest operations.
Danger! Do not pass any vehicle loading timber until you have been told it is safe to do so.
Footpaths are for walkers only.
Cycle with care and come back again.

THE MOUNTAIN CODE
Issued by the Mountaineering Club of Great Britain

Know how to use a map and compass
Know the weather signs and local forecast
Plan within your capabilities
Know simple first aid and the symptoms of exposure
Know the mountain distress signal
Never go alone
Leave written word of your route and report on your return
Take waterproofs, woollens and a survival bag
Take a map, compass, torch and food.

ABBREVIATIONS

Compass points and directions are abbreviated throughout to N, S, E, W, R & L. 'SP' stands for sign post. When it refers to altitude, metre(s) is abbreviated to m; otherwise metres in full refers to distance.

1: CORRIEYAIRACK PASS

Location/Start & Finish: The classic Corrieyairack Pass lies in the south-western sector of the Monadhliath Mountains between Fort Augustus and Laggan/Kingussie.

There are three alternatives for the crossing:

a) Fort Augustus, MR 34/379092 – Melgarve 34/468959 or Garva Bridge 35/522947 or Laggan 35/615943, all various extensions of the same old military road.

b) Return journey. Melgarve or Garva Bridge – Fort Augustus and back in one day.

c) Two-day foray. Laggan – Fort Augustus on Day 1, then return on Day 2, with the option to use one of the Fort Augustus based rides, routes 25 or 26 as an intermediate entertainment.

Route: a) Start on the A82 in Fort Augustus, nominally at the bridge over the Caledonian Canal, 50 metres S of the main car park. (Space for 100 cars, tariff 60p for up to 10 hours in 2003). Over the Corrieyairack Pass to Melgarve, where the rough-stuff ends, 24.29 km (15.09 miles) (space for two cars), or Garva Bridge, 30.25 km (18.79 miles) (parking for six cars), or Laggan, 41.76 km (25.95 miles). This unidirectional ride, hopefully with any wind behind you – anything from W through NW to N, which are the prevailing directions, can be of assistance - is the best option for a first time crossing, and being met by a vehicle at the far end, anywhere from Laggan to Melgarve is an excellent idea.

b) Some of the Scottish hard riders use the double crossing from Melgarve to Fort Augustus and back in a day as an indicator of early season fitness, total distance 48.58 km (30.19 miles), most of it very tough and exposed going, with only 3.10 km (1.93 miles) of tarmac between the end of Wade's military road and Fort Augustus included in the total. Only for the most competent and very fit do it in this direction because the zigzags in Corrie Yairack are unrideable uphill and only marginally better down! Do the walking first!

  c) If you plan to arrive by train the two-day foray is suggested, which of course could be extended to include the Great Glen and/or Fort Augustus based routes, or possible return to central Scotland via Fort William and the classic train journey over Rannoch Moor. (See Appendix 1 - Links & mini-tours.)

Maps: Landrangers 34 Fort Augustus &   35 Kingussie. The short options, Fort Augustus – Melgarve and vice versa are entirely on sheet 34. (ROUTE MAP ON PAGES 16 & 17)

Gradings: Strenuous 17/18, (b) Very strenuous 19! (c) Strenuous both days, 18.

Approaches: Nearest train station to Fort Augustus is Spean Bridge 36.8 km (22.9 miles) to the S, nearest to Laggan is Newtonmore 12.9 km (8.0 miles) to the E. Approach by car from the Edinburgh direction is best via A9 to Dalwhinnie, then A889 to the junction with A86 at the Monadhliath Hotel where turning R will take you N to Laggan and the eastern approaches, or L will carry you W to Spean Bridge, then NE on A82 to Fort Augustus. From Glasgow follow A82 all the way to Fort William and on to Fort Augustus.

Facilities: Running water is the only refreshment available on the entire route! Fort Augustus is well geared for travellers, with a full range of accommodation, and especially good grub at the Lock Inn. Try the Mallaig haddock. Tell Danny we sent you! There's a village store in Laggan, the Monadhliath Hotel about a mile S, and a bunkhouse and amazing cream cakes at the pottery on A889 at Middleton, M R 35/620937.

There are toilets at the main car park in Fort Augustus and opposite the village shop in Laggan. Nearest bike shops are in Fort William, Aviemore or Inverness.

Route description: Option (a): Depart S on the A82 from the bridge over the Caledonian Canal in Fort Augustus, then swing L past the abbey entrance within 100m onto B862, huge SP Errogie and others. Follow this narrow road for 1.30 km (0.81 mile) past the extreme southern end of Loch Ness, looking to turn R when B862 swings L, uphill.

Turn sharp hairpin R, uphill onto narrower single-track road, still tarmac. No SP for us, and follow this SW for 1.80 km (1.12 miles) past Ardachy Lodge and Culachy House, looking to turn L into a gorse and broom-lined track immediately before a white cottage on the L. Running total 3.10 km (1.93 miles). This is the start of the section of General Wade's road we use.

Turn L into the rough track, Scottish Rights of Way Society SP Corrieyairack Pass. Fort Augustus to Laggan. Initially big round stones to gate with home-made sign! Intermittent water damage to track, but all clear after 400m, then you simply follow the main track for a further 1.80 km (1.12 miles) keeping R above Culachy Falls (which you can't see!) into wilder country altogether.

After 4.90 km (3.04 miles) keep L at Knollbuck road end, the road on the R leading only to the transmission mast. Head down towards the trees. Look for the old road weaving its way up the far side of the glen. Several apparent options, but once you cross the burn the smoothest road becomes obvious. Tough sustained climbing to Creag Dhubh col after 2.75 km (1.71 miles).

Creag Dhubh col, 320m, 7.65 km (4.73 miles) gone. Under the power lines, briefly downhill, then up again and around to Blackburn. Big undulations for 2.54 km (1.58 miles). Starts to get lonely!

Black Burn reached after 10.19 km (6.33 miles). Straight across the burn then swing L and back up to the pylons again, eventually swinging L down to the venerable Bailey bridge (1961) at Allt Lagan a' Bhainne after 2.87 km (1.78 miles). The original Wade bridge is upstream in the trees. Repairs imminent on several of the bridges - follow any signs.

Total of 13.06 km (8.12 miles) ridden at Allt Lagan a' Bhainne. Steeply up through the hairpins, around to Allt Coire Uchdachan and same again. Onwards into the upper reaches of the Corrieyairack Pass itself, 4.56 km (2.83 miles) to the summit. Still good stony surface and great views, but in mist those dreaded pylons become good friends.

Corrieyairack Pass Summit, 764m, after 17.62 km (10.95 miles). Straight on past the little building and power lines at 775m, then steeply downhill to the top of the zigzags. Take special care if misty, you could be going far too fast! (Believe me - DP!) Follow the only track for 6.67 km (4.14 miles) to the sleeper bridge at Melgarve, but keep an eye out for the older zigzags in the early stages. There used to be 18 traverses, now reduced to 13. Rough in the zigzags, even rougher at the bottom after a hard winter. Wet fords! Road improves as you approach Melgarve.

Melgarve bridge, just beyond the bothy, 24.29 km (15.09 miles) gone. Use the bridge - ford hazardous even when frozen - then follow the undulating single-track tarmac down to the ancient Garva Bridge - leave the gate as you find it - turn L at the concrete bridge over the canal near Glen Shirra reservoir, past the Spey Dam, down across the River Spey again and on to Laggan. Total distance 41.76 km (25.95 miles).

There is something very special about crossing the Corrieyairack, possibly ethereal. Perhaps due to the circumstances surrounding its construction, possibly the exposure of the route and location deep in the Highlands, possibly the tales and superstitions relating to its past. Judge for yourself.

Options (b) and (c). Approaching the pass from Laggan in the east, both bikes and cars use the same single-track tarmac road. There is an

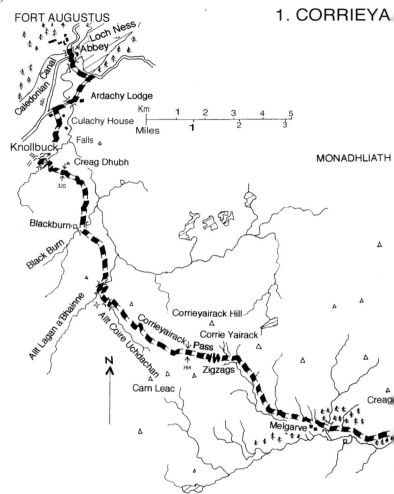

1. CORRIEYA

FORT AUGUSTUS
Loch Ness
Abbey
Caledonian Canal
A82
Ardachy Lodge
Culachy House
Knollbuck
Falls
Creag Dhubh
320
Blackburn
Black Burn
Allit Lagan a'Bhainne
Allt Coire Uchdachan
N
Carn Leac
764
Corrieyairack Hill
Corrie Yairack
Corrieyairack Pass
Zigzags
Melgarve
Creag
MONADHLIATH

Km 1 2 3 4 5
Miles 1 2 3

RACK PASS

MOUNTAINS

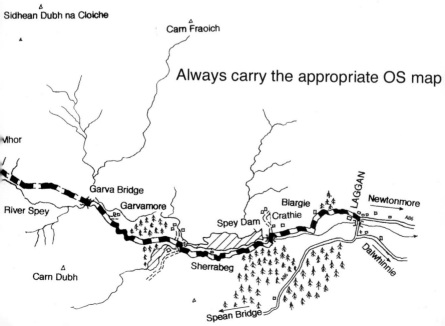

Always carry the appropriate OS map

apparently large parking area 50m W of the village shop at Laggan, but this is the turning area for both the local bus and logging lorries. Park with care.

Depart W, climbing steadily, then down again to the River Spey beyond Blargie farm. The road then turns tight R and runs parallel to the river for 1.66 km (1.03 miles) to the bridge at Crathie road end after a total of 3.86 km (2.40 miles).

Turn L over the bridge - which is the main road - and climb steeply above the Spey Dam. Follow for 3.69 km (2.29 miles) past Sherrabeg and a lonely little remnant of an original Wade bridge to the new concrete bridge over the canal.

Turn R across the concrete bridge, no SP but this is the main road. Follow roughly NW to Garva Bridge, reached after a total of 11.51 km (7.15 miles).

Turn R over the ancient Garva Bridge, or if you are starting from here simply cross the bridge and head WNW then W to Melgarve, where the rough-stuff starts.

Navigation is easy from here, there are no choices.

Melgarve is reached after a further 9.92 km (6.16 miles).

Another, lumpy, 6.67 km (4.14 miles) takes you to the summit of the pass, then it's a mainly downhill 14.52 km (9.02 miles) of quite good stony road to the tarmac beyond Culachy House. The descent into and climb out of the little glen SW of Culachy House seems a bit unfair, but that's mountain biking for you! If you are doing the two-way tester it's even more unfair!

On reaching the tarmac at the white cottage you will see that a tempting gnarly little path continues the line of Wade's Road, but this only runs for 210m then you would need to use a fast section of the A82. Turning R past Ardachy Lodge, then L onto the B862 is a safer approach to Fort Augustus. Total distance 41.76 km (25.95 miles).

Garva Bridge: The gate is often open, especially in winter. Leave as you find it. Look out for it as you approach at the end of the long straight downhill.

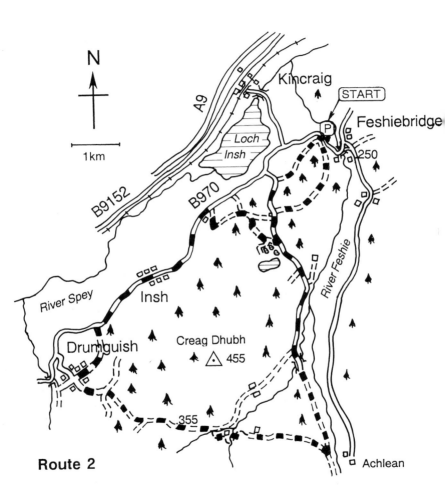

Route 2

2: INSHRIACH FOREST

Location: 9.6 km (6.0 miles) S of Aviemore, 12.8 km (8.0 miles) NE of Kingussie, on eastern side of River Spey. Start/Finish at free Forestry Enterprise car park, map ref. NH 849 046, on B970, 800 m. NW of Feshiebridge. Space for 10 cars.

Route: 27 km (16.8 miles) of which 18.4 km (11.4 miles) is off-road, in the undulating afforested countryside of Strathspey, but two unbridged river crossings, before and after Baileguish demand great caution and skill in wet weather.

Map: Landranger 35 Kingussie & Monadhliath Mountains.

Grading: Moderate 8. Surface 2 (short section 5), ascent 2, general conditions 2, length 2.

Approaches: From S use A9 to B9150 for Newtonmore, then A86 to Kingussie, where turn R onto B970. Feshiebridge is 13.7 km (8.5 miles) NE of Kingussie. From N use A9 to Aviemore, then B970 across River Spey and SW to Feshiebridge. Nearest railway station is Aviemore.

Facilities: B & B available at Balcraggan, Feshiebridge. Hotels, bunkroom and combined Post Office/Tourist Information Centre/general store in Kincraig NW of Feshiebridge, also food and bike hire at Loch Insh Watersports Centre nearby (February - October). Hostel accommodation in Glen Feshie at NH 849 009 marked as Balachroik on the map. (Free porridge!)

Route description:
Turn R out of the car park onto B970 then L into the track at

Balcraggan within 200 metres, which divides almost immediately beyond the green gate. Take the L fork and follow through the forest to the end - about 2.4 km (1.5 miles), where you turn L again onto the metalled road. Follow this road S for 3.2 km (1.99 miles), past Uath Lochan and Ballintean to the bridge over the Allt Fhearnasdaill. Just after the bridge the road narrows to a tar track. Go around the gate and continue S up Glen Feshie looking to turn R into the forest after a further 2.4 km (1.49 miles).

The track is signposted as a right of way to Drumguish. After 2 km (1.24 miles) the track emerges onto open moorland. Follow the track W, but after 400 metres it becomes rather indistinct as it turns S across pasture land to the ford across the Allt na Caoileig. Aim for the abandoned croft of Baileguish then swing N to another ford. Wet feet are almost inevitable!

Once across Allt Chomhraig turn L onto a rising forest track into the wood. The gate should be open. After 1.6 km (0.99 mile) fork R onto the old forest track and follow for 800 metres to the modern forest road. Turn R and head downhill for 1.2 km (0.75 mile) to a crossroads where you turn L. Within a few hundred metres the track leaves the forest, through a gate in the deer fence and across the moor to Drumguish.

Turn R at the crossroads by the telephone box, then straight on along the forest edge when tarmac ends. After about 800 metres there is a deer fence, do not go through the gate but turn L down the rough track to join B970 at NH 798 006. Turn R along B970 for 4.0 km (2.48 km) through Insh towards Feshiebridge.

About 200 metres beyond Lynachlaggan turn R onto the forest track that rises back behind the house. There is a short ascent over 800 metres, then at the T-junction turn R up the ravine. At the end of this track there is a Forest Enterprise car park (and marked trails around Uath Lochan for walkers only!) Turn L to return to the road, then L again for 1.6 km (0.99 mile) to Balnespick. Just before the road descends past the farm turn R onto the track that leads along the side of the woodland. Brilliant fast swooping downhill approach - don't overshoot! At the cattle-shed the track divides, take the R fork, then the track splits again, carry on through the right-hand gate. After less than 800 metres the track enters the wood. Go straight on, then finally turn R at the B970 to return to the car park.

Places of interest: Ruthven Barracks is an impressive Ancient Monument, 3 km (1.9 miles) W of Drumguish.

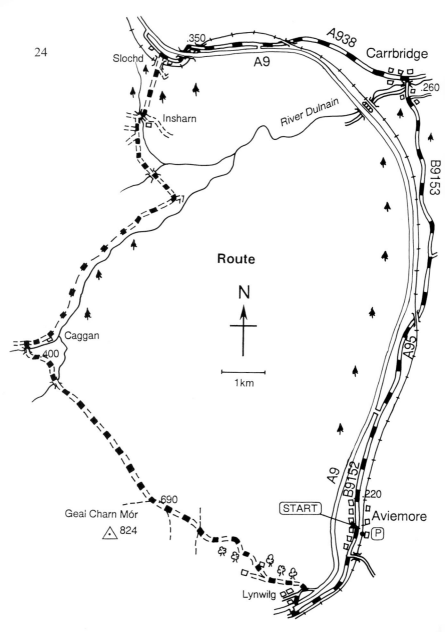

Slochd

.350

A9

A938

Carrbridge

.260

Insharn

River Dulnain

B9153

Route

N

Caggan

1km

.400

A95

A9

B9T52

220

START

Aviemore

P

.690

Geal Charn Mór

△ 824

Lynwilg

3: THE BURMA ROAD

Location/Start & Finish: The ride starts and finishes in Aviemore, 47 km (29 miles) S of Inverness, 188 km (117 miles) N of the Forth Bridge. There are several car parks in Aviemore, some free. Try the free riverside car park opposite the Aviemore Bunk House and Old Bridge Inn at NH 895 117 in Dalfaber Road, parallel to the main street but on the E side of the railway. To get there turn E onto B970 opposite La Taverna restaurant at the S end of town, SP Coylumbridge, cross the River Spey, then first L down to the Bunk House, signposted Strathspey Railway.

Route: 40 km (24.9 miles) of which 20 km (12.4 miles) is off-road on well defined tracks. One of the most popular rides from Aviemore. The old military road rises horrendously steeply from Lynwig, just S of Aviemore, to an altitude of 698 m. This is followed by a swooping, fast 4 km (2.5 mile) descent to the River Dulnain. The route then follows the river to Slochd and returns on metalled roads via Carrbridge.

Maps: Landrangers 35 Kingussie & Monadhliath Mountains, and 36 Grantown & Aviemore.

Grading: Strenuous 16. Surface 3, ascent 5, general conditions 2 and 5, length 3.

Approaches: Aviemore lies just off the A9 Perth-Wick trunk road 128 km (76 miles) N of Perth. Look for the signs once you pass Kingussie if travelling from the S, or the Carrbridge/Aviemore junction when approaching from the N. Aviemore railway station is opposite the riverside parking, simply start the ride from the station by heading S out of town on B9152 towards Kingussie.

Facilities: Aviemore is well geared to visitors with a range of accommodation to suit every taste, and more than one bike shop.

The Slochd Ski Centre/The Cycle Factory at NH 848 238, which is half way round the route has the best repair facilities in the Highlands, cottages for rent and a café. The Old Bakery Coffee Shop in Carrbridge serves excellent coffee and has huge slices of cake, whilst the Struan Hotel does excellent bar meals - fish and chips recommended.

Route description: From the Old Bridge Inn head S up the hill to B970, turn R across the River Spey then T-junction L at B9152, SP Kingussie (A9) and head SW. After 2.38 km (1.48 miles) turn R, SP Perth (A9), up to and carefully across the A9, turning R SP Inverness, then L within 50 metres SP Lynwilg. Follow the old road past the farm looking to turn L immediately beyond the bridge after 0.49 km (0.30 mile) SP Alltnachiche. There is also a Scottish Rights of Way Society plaque Right of Way to Carrbridge via the Burma Road and the River Dulnain. 21 km (13 m).

After 0.79 km (0.49 mile) of narrow pristine tarmac fork R at the entrance to Alltnachiche onto rougher tarmac to big double gates (usually locked) with a high awkward stile. This track rises very steeply uphill through an area of pine and birch trees, the tarmac disappearing after 360 metres. This is the start of the Burma Road and a relentless well-defined climb of 4.34 km (2.70 miles) to the top of the pass. The road is resurfaced from time to time, is always firm but can be gritty. The summit is marked by a memorial plaque to Alaistair Polson M.M., followed by the fast descent to the Allt Ghiuthais. A short climb and 1.20 km (0.75 mile) downhill completes the descent to the River Dulnain where you turn R.

The track now follows the river to Caggan. From here there is a grassy track past the farm buildings at Eil. This continues, following the river to a ford over a river tributary. The crossing is easier about 20 metres upstream but a wet foot is still likely. The hard track then resumes.

Just before the junction at Mon. (a slender monument) there is a deer fence, take the L fork. The track now leads roughly N through an area of conifer trees. At the T-junction at the end turn R towards Insharn. Within 100 metres, and before reaching the farmhouse, turn L onto a forest track. This track runs above a further small river to the Ski and Mountain Bike Centre at Slochd. Cross the railway bridge and continue through the large car park to the minor road, where you turn R.

This minor road heads E under the A9, over the railway and soon merges with A938. In parts it is now also National Cycle Route 7. Follow for 6.4 km (4.0 miles) to Carrbridge, where turn R and return to Aviemore along B9153, A95 and eventually B9152, a distance of 10.40 km (6.50 miles).

Places of interest: Carrbridge, in particular the Landmark Visitor Centre. Strathspey Railway, in the course of being extended (October 2003).

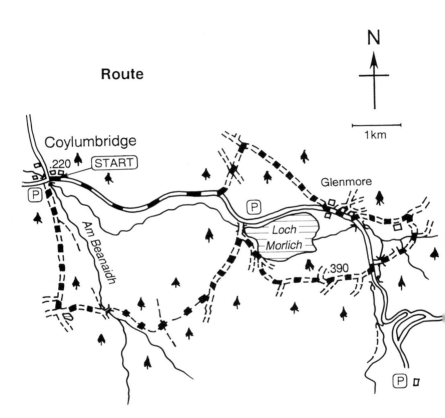

Route

N

1km

Coylumbridge

.220 START

P

Am Beanaidh

Glenmore

P

Loch Morlich

.390

P

4: ROTHIEMURCHUS ESTATE AND LOCH MORLICH

Location/Start & Finish: The ride starts from B970 at Coylumbridge 3 km (2 miles) ESE of Aviemore, nominally at the entrance to Rothiemurchus Camp & Caravan Park at NH 915 106, where there is roadside parking for three cars to the W of the junction. There is also room for six cars at the little Lairig Ghru car parks 300 metres S along the track used by the route at NH 915 103. Once you stick your nose into the track at the side of the Camp & Caravan Park you will see a board Lairig Ghru car park 100 m., then another after 100 m! The spaces beside the burned out cottage have no official charge, but a donation in the red box would seem appropriate.

Route: 26 km (16 miles) of which 23 km (14 miles) off-road. A delightful low-level circular tour beneath the Cairngorm Mountains.
NB: This route can be combined with route 7, Glenmore & Abernethy Forests, to provide a 51 km (32 mile) tour.

Maps: Landranger 36 Grantown & Aviemore, or Outdoor Leisure 3 (1:25,000) The Cairngorms.

Grading: Moderate 8. Surface 2, ascent 2, general conditions 2, length 2.

Approaches: From both N and S use A9 to Aviemore, then B970 from the S end of town, signposted Coylumbridge. The Camp & Caravan Park is on the S side of the road immediately before the COYLUMBRIDGE sign, 2.81 km (1.74 miles) from the B9152 in Aviemore. Nearest railway station is Aviemore.

Facilities: Rothiemurchus Camp & Caravan Park has all the usual facilities including a shop. The whole area is well geared to visitors.

Route description: From the roadside parking area head S along the track which runs parallel with the edge of the caravan park. There is a signpost hidden in the bushes marking it as a right of way through to Braemar. Follow the track for 3.22 km (2.00 miles) initially following cyclists signs for Glen Einich, through the woodland and out onto an area of open moor. There are four gates to be negotiated along this stretch, one of which (at the cattle grid) has the potential to be locked, but there is an accompanying stile.

At the cross-tracks (NH 916 079), where there are many signs, turn L passing a small loch on your R (which was virtually dry at the end of the 2003 summer). Continue E and cross the river using the Cairngorm Club Iron Footbridge. The wide pathway provides a good cycling surface as it follows the river S and then swings to head NE.

About 2.40 km (1.50 miles) beyond the footbridge there is a deer fence which can be crossed via a high stile – note the convenient dog flap.

Continue on until the path meets a wide track that serves Rothiemurchus Lodge. Turn L down the track, then after almost 1.60 km (0.99 mile) and just before reaching Loch Morlich, turn R onto another forest track. After fording the narrow stream go through the gate in the deer fence into Glenmore Forest Park. Once through the gate turn almost immediately R. Follow this forest road as it winds up and around the tiny Serpents Loch. Continue on, following the blue-topped ski marker posts. At the T-junction (NH 972083) turn R. Continue E to the junction with the tar road that gives access to the Ski Centre.

Turn L along the road for 100 metres, then turn R onto the path that leads into the wood and across the river via a very narrow wooden bridge. The path soon widens to become a track. Follow the track as it swings to the N, still following blue-topped posts. About 800 metres beyond the wooden bridge there is a further river to ford. This can be quite deep but there is a footbridge 50 metres upstream.

Continue N to the T-junction with the Ryvoan Pass track (NH 992 097). Turn L. After 600 metres there is a green gate. Continue straight on along the tar road and past the National Outdoor Training Centre. At the junction with the ski road turn R. After 400 metres turn R onto the track opposite the Glenmore café and shop.

This track heads NW up into the forest. Turn L after 2.40 km (1.49 miles) at the T-junction near Badaguish. Follow this track downhill, across the cross-tracks, to the ski road, where you turn R. It is then about 3.20 km (1.99 miles) back to Coylumbridge.

Places of interest: Rothiemurchus Estate is fully geared up to cater for tourists. In addition to the Visitor Centre, café and shops, there are way-marked forest walks, a nature trail, farm tours, estate safaris, loch and river fishing, clay pigeon shooting – even for novices, and a fish-farm.

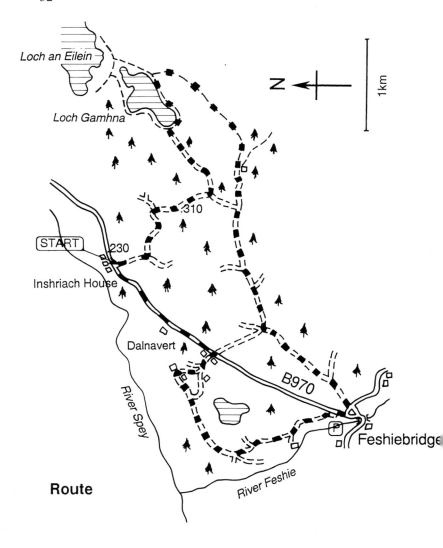

Loch an Eilein

Loch Gamhna

N ←

1km

START 230

Inshriach House

310

Dalnavert

River Spey

B970

River Feshie

Feshiebridge

Route

5: MOOR OF FESHIE

Location/Start & Finish: The Start, on the B970, 400 metres S of Inshriach Garden Centre is 7.2 km (4.5 miles) S of Aviemore and 16.0 km (9.9 miles) NE of Kingussie, map ref. NH 871 071. Space for two neatly parked cars in wide forest entry.

Route: 15.0 km (9.3 miles) of which 12.8 km (7.95 miles) are off-road. A mainly gentle and low-level mixed ride abutting the western slopes of the Cairngorm Mountains, but you may still get your feet wet!

Map: Landranger 35 Kingussie & Monadhliath Mountains.

Grading: Moderate 6. Surface 2 (short section 4), ascent 2, general conditions 1. length 1.

Approaches: From both N and S the A9 to Aviemore is best, B970 from Aviemore to Inverdruie, then SW for 4.8 km (2.99 miles) still on B970 to Inshriach. The triangular junction in Inverdruie is signposted Feshiebridge. Nearest railway station is Aviemore.

Facilities: There are no facilities on the route. Aviemore should be able to fulfil all your needs! Inshriach Garden Centre has a tearoom pitched at the senior horticultural brigade!

Route description: From the forest access S of Inshriach Garden Centre (opposite a white wicket gate) follow the track S up into the woods. Fork L when the track divides after 310 metres, riding down then up onto the stiffest climb of the ride. Ignore the track on the L after a further 590 metres and head S, then from the top of the rise it is downhill past another road on the L. After another 0.93 km (0.58 mile) turn L onto a narrower track when the road swings R. This becomes more technical the farther you go, culminating in a lumpy root-strewn approach to the gap in the boundary wall after 1.19 km (0.74 mile). We are told the gap is official. Follow the path down to Loch Gamhna.

At the edge of the loch turn R, then as the path nears the northern end of the loch turn R onto another path that heads SSW down the glen. The path can be muddy, but after 1.20 km (0.75 mile) you must ford the Allt Coire Follais. When the water is high it is easier to cross about 50 metres upstream.

At the far side of the river the path widens to a track; continue W past the bothy, then straight on into the wood. The gate seems to have been permanently removed, but there is also a stile. After just over 1.60 km (0.99 mile) turn L at the cross-tracks, then after a further 1.60 km (0.99 mile) you reach a junction with a minor road. Turn R to B970, R again on the main road, then look for a track on the L within 250 metres. Follow this track to a green gate and continue NNW into the forest.

After 800 metres fork L when the track divides at a small clearing, then turn R onto a smaller pebbled track after another 400 metres. This surface gradually eases, then follow the field edge, and after 800 metres the surface becomes a firm track. Continue straight on at the T-junction and through the deer fence gate at the edge of the forest. Turn R at the flagpole and follow the track uphill over the cattle grid to B970. Turn L and follow the main road back to Inshriach.

Places of interest: Ruthven Barracks (line drawing opposite) is an impressive ancient monument. It is 3 km west of Drumguish.

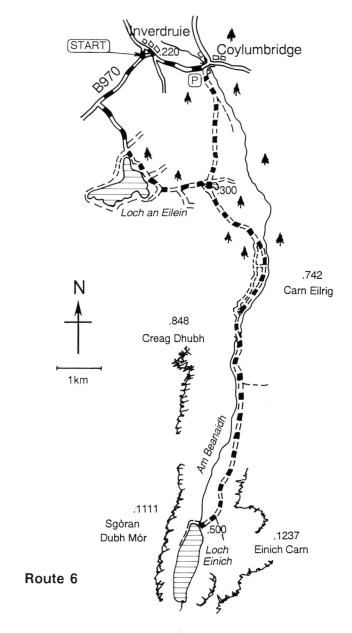

Route 6

6: GLEN EINICH

Location/Start & Finish: Glen (or Gleann) Einich lies 10.0 km (6.0 miles) SSE of Aviemore, accessed through Rothiemurchus Estate. Start from the sunken village car park at Inverdruie, lodged in the B970 triangle at NH 901 109 opposite Rothiemurchus Visitor Centre.

Route: Largely an 'out-and-back' ride, 29.0 km (18.0 miles) of which 24.0 km (14.9 miles) is off-road. Arguably the most dramatic rideable glen in the Cairngorms, Glen Einich is squashed between the great bulk of Braeriach to the E and the cliffs of Sgoran Dubh to the W, towering above Loch Einich. NOTE: Deer culling takes place, usually between 1 September and about 20 October each year, there will be a sign to this effect on the first gate you encounter, asking you to "keep to recognised paths", which therefore does not effect the ride.

Maps: Landranger 36 Grantown & Aviemore, or Outdoor Leisure 3 (1:25,000) The Cairngorms.

Grading: Energetic 12. Surface 3, ascent 3, general conditions 4, length 2.

Approaches: From both N and S use A9 to Aviemore, then B970 from the S end of town signposted "Inverdruie, Coylumbridge". Inverdruie is 1.2 km (0.75 mile) SE of Aviemore. Look for the Rothiemurchus Visitor Centre on the L. Nearest railway station is Aviemore, where the GNER sleeper train stops. (Info. September 2003).

Facilities: The area has everything! But, there is nothing at all in the wild country S of Coylumbridge!

Route description: From the car park at Inverdruie head E along

B970 for 1.60 km (0.99 mile) to Coylumbridge. Look to turn R into the entrance of Rothiemurchus Camp & Caravan Park, but use the track that heads S along the side of the site. It is signposted as a right of way to Braemar and also to the Lairig Ghru car park.

Follow this track S for 3.22 km (2.00 miles) following Rothiemurchus cyclists signs for Glen Einich. There are four gates, the second of which has the potential to be locked, but there is a stile.

At the cross-tracks continue SSE past the small lochan, which was all but dry in September 2003. The gate just beyond has a gap at the side allowing free passage. After 2.04 km (1.27 miles) where the track divides at a ford, take the lower left-hand route which is signposted for cyclists. This junction marks the start of a very gentle but steady climb over the next 5.60 km (3.38 miles).

At first the track clings to the hillside some metres above the river but after about 1.60 km (0.99 mile) the glen opens out. A plank bridge has been provided for the river crossing at NH 924 043, but some burns further up the glen require careful negotiation. This bridge was removed for repairs on 22 July 2003, but should have been replaced by the summer of 2004. Once Loch Einich is reached there is little point in trying to cycle round the shore – the gritty sand is impossible to ride. Enjoy the view and then return down the glen.

When you reach the cross-tracks at the small lochan, turn L. After 1.20 km (0.75 mile) turn R at the T-junction and cross the river on wooden planks. Follow the track around the shore of Loch an Eilein.

There are two further gates to negotiate before reaching a car park. From here follow the tar track NW to the B970, then turn R. It is 1.6 km (0.99 mile) back to Inverdruie.

Places of interest: Rothiemurchus Estate offers plenty of outdoor activities for all ages as well as the Visitor Centre, café and shops. Strathspey Steam Railway runs between Aviemore and Boat of Garten.

The small loch en route to Glen Einich

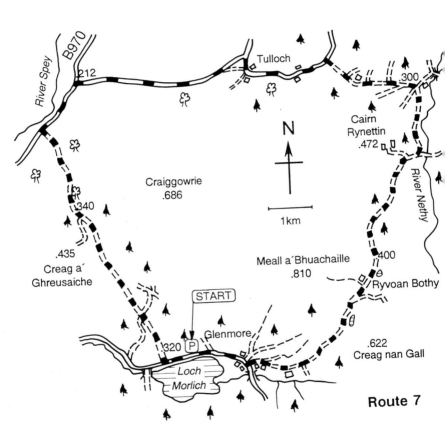

River Spey

B970

.212

Tulloch

.300

Cairn
Rynettin
.472

River Nethy

N

Craiggowrie
.686

1km

.340

.435
Creag a´
Ghreusaiche

Meall a´Bhuachaille
.810

.400

Ryvoan Bothy

START

Glenmore

.320 P

.622
Creag nan Gall

Loch
Morlich

Route 7

7: GLENMORE & ABERNETHY FORESTS

Location/Start & Finish: Glenmore Forest Park is 8 km (5 miles) E of Aviemore. The ride starts from the N shore of Loch Morlich, where there are a number of car parks (£1.00 for all day – Sept. 2003). The one at NH 972 099 is favourite.

Route: 29 km (18 miles) of which 22.4 km (13.9 miles) is off-road. A classic circular tour which connects two protected areas of Caledonian Pine Forest using the Ryvoan and Slugan Passes. During 2003, a shared pedestrian/cycle track, which will keep you clear of through traffic, was under construction parallel to the ski road skirting Loch Morlich.

Map: Landranger 36 Grantown & Aviemore

Grading: Moderate 10. Surface 2 and 3, ascent 2, general conditions 3, length 2.

Approaches: From both N and S aim for Aviemore, using A9 or A95 from Moray coast. From the S end of Aviemore turn SE for Coylumbridge on B970, then continue E for a further 5.7 km (3.5 miles) to Loch Morlich when the B970 turns N. This is the main approach to Glenmore and the Cairngorm Ski Centre, very easy to follow.

Facilities: There are eateries, caravan and camping parks spread all along the ski road, plus a full range of year-round facilities in Aviemore. Nearest railway station is Aviemore.

Route description: From the N shore of Loch Morlich head E along the ski road. Just past the Visitor Centre and campsite turn L onto the tar track, SP Glenmore Lodge. About 100 metres beyond the Lodge, the tar seal finishes. Continue roughly NE through the green gate and up into the Ryvoan Pass, where there are some impressive Caledonian pines. If you want to pause by Lochan Uaine, please dismount and approach on foot as it is a National Nature Reserve. Just beyond the lochan the track narrows and there is a short climb to Ryvoan Bothy.

Continue N across open moorland and into Abernethy Forest, another Nature Reserve and home to some rare birds including capercaillie. At NH 015 144 the track divides, take the R fork which turns E and then back to the N. At the cross-tracks just short of Forest Lodge continue straight across, then L at the T-junction to head W to Cuchanlupe. Swing NW at Cuchanlupe to a T-junction at the public road.

Turn L and follow the tar road for 1.92 km (1.19 miles) to Tulloch. About 300 metres beyond the telephone box turn L onto the forest track which begins just before the modern house. This track rejoins tarred road after 800 metres. Turn L and continue W for 3.48 km (2.16 miles) to the B970, where you turn L again. After 1.42 km (0.88 mile), as the road emerges from a small plantation of young pine-trees, turn L onto a rough track, SP Milton Cottage.

Where the track divides at Milton, fork R through the gate and begin the climb of the Slugan Pass. As the track rises above the river it can get muddy! At the top, a further gate announces the return to Glenmore Forest Park. Follow the track as it descends S, crossing straight over the cross-tracks, and back to the shore of Loch Morlich.

Places of interest: There are waymarked forest walks in Glenmore Forest Park, watersports available on the loch, and in winter the cross-country skiing is often excellent and conditions far more reliable than at the downhill ski centre.

A frozen Loch Morlich

THE GREAT GLEN – INVERMORISTON TO DRUMNADROCHIT

Always carry the appropriate OS map

8: THE GREAT GLEN, INVERMORISTON TO DRUMNADROCHIT

Location/Start & Finish: Invermoriston sits on the N shore of Loch Ness 40 km (25 miles) SW of Inverness, 56 km (35 miles) NE of Fort William. The ride starts from the new car park (with toilets) on the A82 just S of the junction with A887 at Invermoriston, map reference NH 421 167, and finishes at the main car park in Drumnadrochit, map reference NH 508 298.

Route: 23.26 km (14.45 miles) in total, of which 15.70 km (9.76 miles) is off-road, all following the modified Great Glen Cycle Route, which is waymarked. The newest section of the GGCR from NH 494 236 to the minor road near Grotaig can be considered as the sting in the tail of the off-road section, but you can also treat the final tarred descent through the zigzags to Borlum Bridge as a fitting climax The last few hundred metres into Drumnadrochit simply follows the A82.

Maps: Landrangers 26 Inverness & Loch Ness, and 34 Fort Augustus.

Grading: Energetic 14. Surface 1, 2 and 4, ascent 5, general conditions 4, length 2.

Approaches: A82 from N and S is the only route in, apart from the A887 from Kyle of Lochalsh. No convenient rail head.

Facilities: Invermoriston has a hotel and shop, Drumnadrochit has cafés, hotels, B & Bs and filling station. Loch Ness youth hostel at Alltsigh is about halfway along the off-road section of the route.

Route description: Turn R out of the car park at Invermoriston, L into A887 in front of the hotel, SP Kyle of Lochalsh, Great Glen Cycle

Route, then look to turn hairpin R immediately past the Clog & Craft Shop into a narrow, steep tarmac climb. The GGCR sign is opposite the clog shop, but nearly totally obscured by vegetation. After 960 metres (and 120 m of ascent!) – this being used as the Loch Ness Monster Hill Climb at the opening of the GGCR – turn R onto forest track, the gradient easing somewhat!

After 800 metres go through a deer gate, then fork R. After a further 150 metres turn off the track and descend a specially constructed path to the lower forest road. Turn L and follow NE above Loch Ness for about 1.6 km (1.0 mile) – past a tiny Victorian rock cave – then the track levels out and continues for about 2.4 km (1.5 miles) to Alltsigh, where you can descend to the youth hostel and A82.

Just after crossing the gully – the Allt Saigh – about 200 metres before the road, turn L onto a further forest track. This is the start of the 3.52 km (2.19 miles) climb to an altitude of 310 m. After 2.56 km (1.59 miles) there is a L turn which continues the climb through a km of switchbacks. Where the track divides at the top, turn R. From here there is another gentle climb!

The high level track then continues NE through mature trees for about 1.6 km (1.0 mile) until another specially constructed path begins the descent. After a further 1.6 km (1.0 mile) the track meets the forest road. Turn L then below Grotaig look for the new section branching off on the L. There are several GGCR signs – missable at speed – leading you into narrow single track along the upper edge of the forestry and into mature deciduous woodland for 1.19 km (0.74 mile) to just E of Grotaig. At the time of writing this track was not shown on O S maps, but is well signposted. Up and down; hard work!

On joining the minor road at the new car park E of Grotaig turn R, and ride NNE on narrow, undulating tarmac for 6.28 km (3.90 miles) to Borlum Bridge. Quite a tough climb back up to 270 m, but a spectacular downhill to Drumnadrochit. Care in the tight bends.

Finally turn L at the A82, Borlum Bridge and follow A82 for 1.28 km (0.79 mile) to Drumnadrochit.

Urquhart Castle

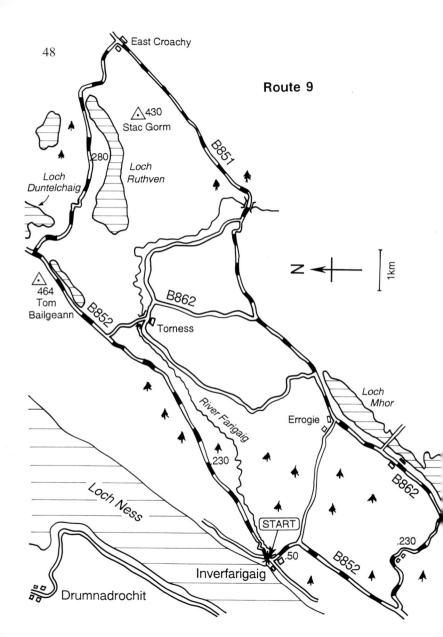

East Croachy

Route 9

△430
Stac Gorm

B851

280

Loch Ruthven

Loch Duntelchaig

△464
Tom Bailgeann

B852

B862

Torness

N

1km

River Farigaig

Errogie

Loch Mhor

230

B862

.230

START

.50

B852

Loch Ness

Inverfarigaig

Drumnadrochit

9: ABOVE INVERFARIGAIG

Location/Start & Finish: Inverfarigaig, on the SE shore of Loch Ness, is 24 km (15 miles) SW of Inverness and 27 km (17 miles) NE of Fort Augustus. Start from the Forest Enterprise car park in Inverfarigaig, map reference NH 521 237, signposted from B852, but hidden behind a beech hedge opposite a Concealed Drive sign. The very narrow road is signposted Errogie.

Route: A circular tour of 43 km (27 miles) on minor roads, some of which could be better classified as tar tracks! From the shore of Loch Ness the route rises through a pretty river gorge to the most dramatic hills and lochs of Stratherick and the RSPB Reserve at Loch Ruthven.

Map: Landranger 35 Kingussie & Monadhliath Mountains

Grading: Energetic 12. Surface 1, ascent 4, general conditions 4, length 3.

Approaches: From Inverness use B862 to Dores, then B852 along the side of Loch Ness. From Fort Augustus follow B862, then B852 through Foyers to Inverfarigaig. Nearest railway station is Inverness, 19 km (12 miles) from the closest point on the route.

Facilities: Inverfarigaig boasts only B & Bs and a public telephone! There is a post office, general store and hotel at both Dores and Foyers. For wider facilities travel to Fort Augustus or Inverness.

Route description: From the Forest Enterprise car park head SE up the Pass of Inverfarigaig. This narrow wooded gorge rises gently as it follows the river. At the bridge after 800 metres keep R into Gleann Liath (no SP for us) and follow this narrow damp road SW. After crossing the huge water pipeline turn L at the next junction, SP Trinloist, Tyndrum. The road now climbs to Loch Mhor.

At the Loch Mhor T-junction (downhill approach) turn L towards Gorthleck, again no SP for us. Follow B862 NE along the loch side through Errogie, SP Dores, Inverness, to the point where the road divides at NH 579 242. Fork R onto B851, SP Daviot into the wilder country of Strath Nairn. The road keeps to the valley floor as it picks its way under the shadow of the craggy hills. After crossing the River Farigaig it swings L, so continue NE for 5.6 km (3.48 miles) to East Croachy.

At East Croachy turn L onto the narrow road to Loch Ruthven, SP RSPB Reserve. The loch, famed for Slavonian Grebes, is squeezed between Stac Gorm and Creag Dhearg, the road following the E then N banks before climbing up to Dalcrombie. There is then a sharp switchback descent to the shore of Loch Duntelchaig and the incredible cliffs of Creag nan Clag, and a short ascent to the junction with B862.

Turn hairpin L and follow B862 as it winds along the shore of Loch Ceo Glais. After 3.61 km (2.24 miles), at the sharp bend beyond the end of the loch, go straight ahead onto the small road, SP Bochruben, Balchraggan. The road soon narrows to little more than a tar track and can be very muddy.

After a little over 1.6 km (1.0 mile) you reach the forest edge. Ride past forest on the R, then on the L. It slowly descends through Balchraggan and past Ballaggan, finishing with a fast, twisting downhill to Inverfarigaig. Turn L at the bottom back to the Forest car park.

Places of interest: There is a forest life exhibition centre and waymarked forest walks from the Forest Enterprise car park at Inverfarigaig. The most unusual cliffs of Creag nan Clag are worth riding all the way to see.

Opposite: The junction of Gleann Liath and the Pass of Inverfarigaig

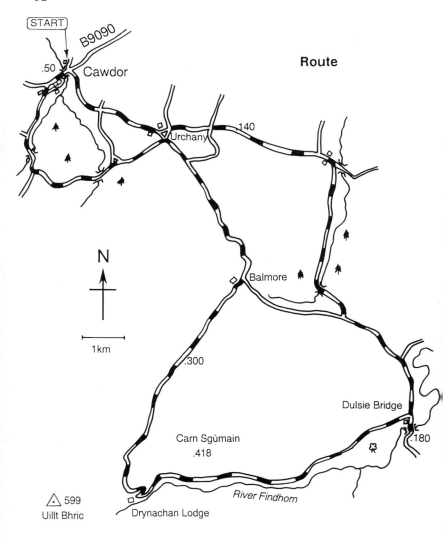

START

B9090

.50 Cawdor

Route

.140 Urchany

N

1km

Balmore

.300

Dulsie Bridge

Carn Sgùmain
.418

.180

△ 599
Uillt Bhric

River Findhorn

Drynachan Lodge

10: CAWDOR AND THE FINDHORN VALLEY

Location/Start & Finish: Cawdor village is 24 km (15 miles) E of Inverness, and 9.6 km (6 miles) SW of Nairn. Space to park is limited, the best place being behind the church at the W end of the village, map reference NH 843 498. The SP Dulsie Bridge is also at the end of this road.

Route: A circular, mainly lowland tour of 42 km (26 miles) on very quiet minor roads through farmland, woodland and plantation forest, across open moorland and along a hilly river valley road.

Map: Landranger 27 Nairn, Forres & surrounding area.

Grading: Moderate 9. Surface 1, ascent 3, general conditions 1 and 2, length 3.

Approaches: From Inverness follow A96 NE for 15.3 km (9.5 miles), then turn R onto B9090 to Cawdor. From Nairn head S on A939 for 3.9 km (2.4 miles), then SW on B9101. Follow handmade SP for Village Shop for best place to park. Nearest railway station is at Nairn, 9.6 km (6.0 miles) from the Start.

Facilities: Shop and pub in Cawdor, otherwise nothing!

Route description: Leave Cawdor on the minor road SP Dulsie Bridge, that heads almost due W from the road at the back of the church at the W end of the village, then swing S and climb to Inchyettle. This road follows the Allt Dearg through Cawdor Wood, then about 300 metres after crossing the river the road swings L, again signposted Dulsie Bridge, and heads E. The very gentle climb continues for a further 800 metres.

Follow the road roughly ENE to the crossroads at Urchany and turn R, SP Clunas, Dulsie, to pass Ordbreck. After passing Mains of Clunas the road climbs out of the forest and up to the Balmore junction. Fork R, SP Drynachan Lodge and climb out onto open moorland. This narrow road undulates across the barren landscape for 4.80 km (2.98 miles).

Just after the road again enters woodland the steep descent to the valley bottom begins. It switchbacks down through woodland for 2.0 km (1.2 miles) to Drynachan Lodge and the farm. At the bottom turn hairpin L and head E following the line of the River Findhorn on a surprisingly hilly narrow road. Ride roughly E for a long 8.11 km (5.04 miles) to the T-junction above Dulsie. The historic Dulsie Bridge, built in 1764, spanning the dramatic Findhorn Gorge, is signposted to the R, but we want to turn L SP Cawdor. A detour down to the bridge adds about 800 metres. From the bridge return to the junction and ride straight on along the Old Military Road as it gently rises N then NW through mixed woodland for a little over 3.20 km (1.99 miles).

At NH 915 443, just beyond the cattle grid, turn R, SP Muckle Burn and descend to the bridge. En route to the T-junction just below Achavraat there are two long straights. Turn L past Achavraat and ride roughly W for 4.64 km (2.88 miles) to Little Urchany. Pass through the hamlet then turn R to return to Cawdor past the castle. In Cawdor turn L across the bridge to finish.

Cawdor Castle

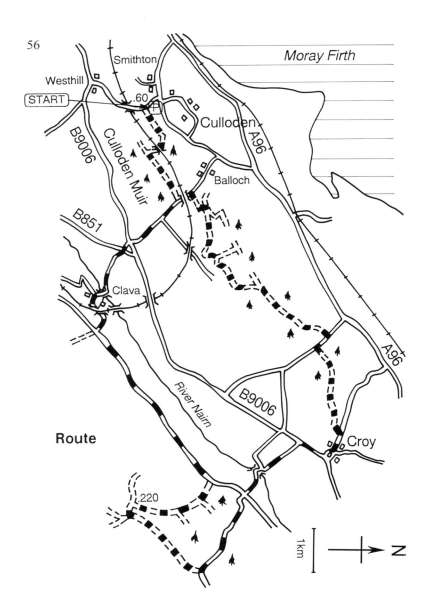

56

Moray Firth

Smithton

Westhill

START

.60 P

Culloden

B9006

Culloden Muir

A96

B851

Balloch

Clava

River Nairn

B9006

Croy

Route

A96

.220

1km

N

11: CULLODEN AND ASSICH FORESTS

Location/Start & Finish: Circular route over Drummossie Muir, immediately E of Inverness and overlooking the Moray Firth Starting and finishing at the Forest Enterprise car park right on the edge of Smithton, map reference NH 717 456, hidden in the trees on the E side of the road. There are Forest Enterprise Culloden and small Balloch via Culloden Wood signs.

Route: 32 km (20 miles) of which 17.6 km (10.9 miles) are off-road. A hilly, mixed route through lowland forest, open farmland and a river valley. Good views across the Moray Firth to the Black Isle and Ross-shire hills. One particularly good descent.

Map: Landranger 27 Nairn, Forres & surrounding area.

Grading: Moderate 10. Surface 1, 2 and 3, ascent 3, general conditions 1 and 2, length 2.

Approaches: From the A9 just S of Inverness via B9006, SP Culloden Muir, then L in Westhill, SP Smithton, Culloden. From A96 ENE of Inverness via Barn Church Road, SP Smithton, Culloden, and then R into Westhill Road SP Culloden Forest Walk. Inverness railway station is 6.4 km (4.0 miles) from the Start.

Facilities: Limited facilities in Smithton and Culloden, but a full range in nearby Inverness.

Route description: Turn R out of the car park and follow the lower track along the backs of the houses through the green gate. After 800 metres turn R and climb through an area of Douglas fir, under the railway line and up to the T-junction where you turn L along the ride. After about 1.6 km (0.99 mile) go straight on through a second gate and ENE to the public road above Balloch. Turn L down the road and back under the railway.

Within 300 metres turn R onto the track just beyond the bus turning area. This track follows the edge to a stand of trees. Go through the gate, along to the stile, then down the path through the gorse bushes for 150 metres. At the junction with the track turn R, then follow the track until it divides when you fork R again.

The track now ascends for 800 metres before turning sharply L. Ignore the ride off to the L – not on O S map – and continue to a T-junction. Turn R and follow for nearly 1.6 km (0.99 mile).

At the bottom of a fast descent you come to a T-junction at NH 757 480, turn R and head NE on what is the major ride through High Wood. The gate at the end is sometimes locked: climb over and turn R along the minor road. After 200 metres turn L into a further track. It's easy to ride around the barrier, then follow the track across the open moor and into the wood.

Here the track becomes a grassy ride which continues all the way to Croy, about 2.4 km (1.5 miles). The gate at the far end should be open. Turn R to Croy village on the minor road. Go past the school and post office, then SW on B9006. Within 800 metres turn L onto the road SP Galcantray. This drops down into the valley of the River Nairn.

A long climb past Rosevalley House starts at the bridge, then straight on through the crossroads and into Assich Forest. About 2.4 km (1.5 miles) beyond the crossroads there is a short descent past a cottage and then a rise over a bridge to a sharp L bend. On the crown of the bend turn R into the unsignposted track. This track quickly emerges from the forest and passes Drummournie farm buildings before setting off in a straight line SW across open fields.

Just before reaching Dalcharn turn R onto a track into the forest. The gate should be open. After 400 metres the track divides. Fork R for a fast descent past Carnach to the hamlet of Balfreish. Watch out for the gate about half way down – it is possible to cycle around it. At the road junction turn L and head SW again.

After almost 4.8 km (3.0 miles) turn R onto the minor road SP Clava. This twisting road descends under the impressive viaduct, down to the river, then up to Culloden Muir. Go straight on at successive B-road crossroads and back to the outward forest track above Balloch, on the L after about 1.6 km (0.99 mile), signposted University of Inverness, Scottish School of Forestry. Retrace the route back to the Smithton car park.

Places of interest: On the route itself are the Clava Stones, impressive Neolithic or Bronze Age stone burial tombs, and Culloden battlefield. Fort George out on the Moray Firth is also worth a visit.

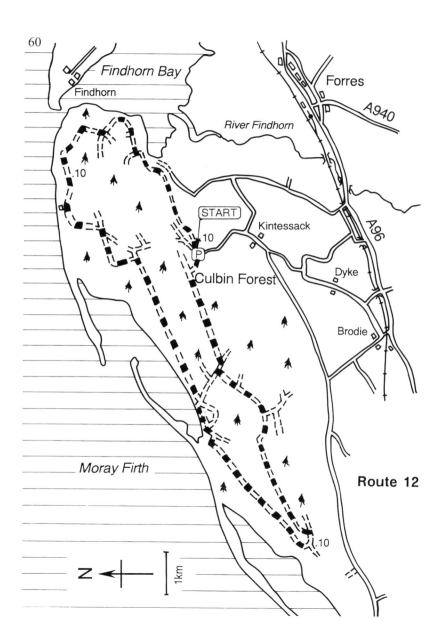

60

Findhorn Bay

Findhorn

Forres

A940

River Findhorn

.10

START

Kintessack

A96

P

Dyke

Culbin Forest

Brodie

Moray Firth

Route 12

.10

N

1km

12: CULBIN FOREST

Location/Start & Finish: Shore of the Moray Firth NNW of Forres, 37 km (23 miles) ENE of Inverness. Start from the Forest Enterprise car park, Culbin, near Wellhill, map reference NH 997 614.

Route: 27.0 km (16.8 miles). A circular off-road tour through Britain's largest system of sand-dunes. The dunes host a Forest Nature Reserve and a Site of Special Scientific Interest. The roads are surfaced with sea-washed pebbles, a most unusual surface.

Map: Landranger 27 Nairn, Forres & surrounding area.

Grading: Moderate 7. Surface 2 and 3, ascent 1, general conditions 1, length 2, but at certain times of year, due to the nature of the terrain, the route can ride a couple of points harder. Judge for yourself.

Approaches: From both the Nairn and Forres directions, Kintessack is well signposted, both at Brodie village and just E of the railway bridge W of Forres. 100 metres beyond Kintessack farm keep L, SP Wellhill, then at the end of the road continue with the forest road for about 400 metres to the car park. Park on the R as soon as you get there, and you will be well placed to depart ENE through the green wooden barrier. Both Nairn and Forres railway stations are 6.4 km (4.0 miles) from the relevant nearest points to the route.

Facilities: There is nothing whatsoever on the route, but both Nairn and Forres are good centres.

Route description: Since this guide was first written Culbin Forest has become host to a number of varying interests, with walkers, botanists, naturalists and of course cyclists. Official mountain bike routes are concentrated at the western end of the forest – as you will encounter – but for an overall tour, this ride will give you a full flavour of Culbin, which can become addictive! There are many, many tracks not shown on ANY map!

Depart ENE past the green wooden barrier (the only exit from the car park without any signs!) then straight on past a short track on the L after 190 metres. Grassy forest twin-track with pebble base, which makes a peculiar noise similar to a puncture! Very leafy, limited views. After 1.90 km (1.18 miles) ride straight on past a grassy single-track on the L, then after another 0.60 km (0.37 mile) swing L with the power lines at a false T-junction and wiggle across to mature trees.

After 0.69 km (0.43 mile) go straight on past a track on the R in the mature trees, straight on past another on the L in 100 metres, then swing L with the main forest road when you reach a field. Continue to weave through the big trees until you reach a junction with a green forest marker post 4 after 1.09 km (0.68 mile). Swing R with the main road again, then keep L past post 3 after 380 metres, and another track on the L 120 metres further on.

You now enter a strange, sparser area, reminiscent of the Siberian taiga! Go straight on at a crossroads near a notice board after 0.81 km (0.50 mile), the road becoming very pebbly. Then swing long, long L and slightly uphill to a fork after another 0.56 km (0.35 mile). Fork R at post 5, straight on again through a mini crossroads after 1.08 km (0.67 mile) and eventually out into an open area overlooking the Moray Firth.

Pause at 'white stump junction' after 1.99 km (1.24 miles), the shortest route to the seaside – a short diversion; aim for the two trees Otherwise, straight on past the open dune area on the R, past another information board, then a track on the R after 0.70 km (0.43 mile). Now S to a crossroads, post 8, surrounded by other tracks after 0.91 km (0.57 miles). Turn R at the crossroads then swing L in a huge arc on soft going for 1.64 km (1.02 miles) to T-junction 13.

There is the possibility of shortening the route here by turning L then swinging S through junctions 12, 9, 11, 10, 2 and finally L at the big crossroads 43 immediately N of the car park. Otherwise, turn R at T-junction 13 and ride WSW for over 3.2 km (2.0 miles) in a straight line to continue the route.

When the road turns sharply L to head S, take the small path on the R which quickly emerges on the shore of the lagoon. A rough grass track leads W along the shore for 500 metres. At the small outcrop of trees turn L through the gorse to rejoin the forest road.

Turn R onto the road and R again after about 250 metres. There can be a deep covering of sand here which makes for hard going. After 3.2 km (2.0 miles) the road turns sharply L. Ignore the turning on the R and follow the road round to the E to begin the return to the car park. Fork L after about 400 metres and follow this main road for 4.8 km (3.0 miles) to a crossroads in Low Wood where you go straight on. Another 600 metres brings you to a T-junction where you turn R, then L after 350 metres. After about 800 metres this track passes the specially constructed wildlife pond, hidden in the trees on the R. About another 800 metres beyond the pond turn R rather than continuing on through the green gate. From here it is 800 metres to the car park.

Places of interest: Brodie Castle is a NTS property, the grounds being open all year, the castle April – October.

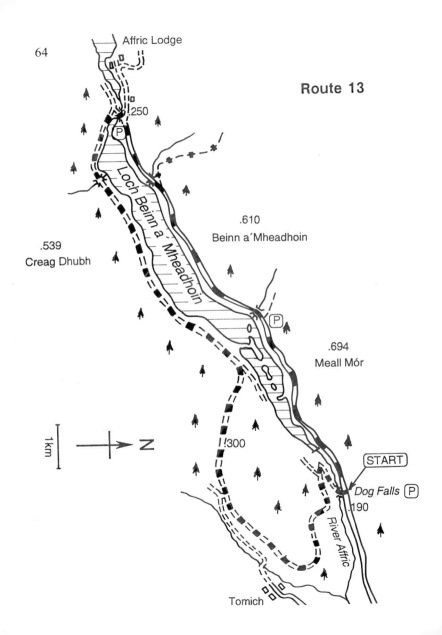

Affric Lodge

Route 13

.250

P

Loch Beinn a'Mheadhoin

.610
Beinn a'Mheadhoin

.539
Creag Dhubh

P

.694
Meall Mór

1km

N

.300

START

Dog Falls P
.190

River Affric

Tomich

13: GLEN AFFRIC

Location/Start & Finish: Glen Affric lies some 45 km (28 miles) as the crow flies SW of Inverness, and slightly more N of Fort William, but the road mileages are somewhat extended. Start & Finish at the Forestry Commission car park for Dog Falls, map reference NH 283 282, 7.68 km (4.77 miles) SW of Cannich. Space for 10 cars.

Route: 34 km (21 miles) of which 22.4 km (13.9 miles) are off-road. A circular tour through the renowned and beautiful Glen Affric with a short excursion into the surrounding hills.

Map: Landranger 25 Glen Carron & Glen Affric

Grading: Energetic 12. Surface 3, ascent 3, general conditions 3, length 3.

Approaches: Cannich is on the A831, 19.2 km (11.9 miles) W of Drumnadrochit and 27.2 km (16.9 miles) SW of Beauly. From Cannich an unclassified road leads SW to Glen Affric. Turn R 3.22 km (2.00 miles) from Cannich, at the power station, SP Glen Affric, the Dog Falls car park is then signposted on the L after a further 4.46 km (2.77 miles). The closest railway station is Muir of Ord, some 32 km (20 miles) from Glen Affric.

Facilities: The hotel in Cannich now offers only hostel/bunkhouse accommodation, there is chalet/caravan/camping site and B & Bs. For more extensive facilities go to Drumnadrochit, Beauly or Muir of Ord.

Route description: From the car park return to the road and turn L, heading WSW up Glen Affric on tarmac. After 1.40 km (0.87 mile), it is possible to divert out onto the Benevean Dam. Return back to the road and continue WSW past Loch Beinn a' Mheadhoin.

From here there is 4 km (2.5 miles) of gentle ascent. The road then undulates without any real change in altitude for several kilometres. After 7.55 km (4.69 miles) you reach the single-track Chisholm Bridge. Do not cross the bridge, instead fork R down through the little ford and follow the rough track along the side of the wood as it turns to the N. Continue with the track as it climbs more gently uphill. There is a deer fence after 1.60 km (0.99 mile). The gate should be open. The views from the gully really open out as the track turns W.

A second deer fence, about 2.4 km (1.5 miles) from the road marks the end of the rideable track. It is possible to follow the river for a further 1.60 km (0.99 mile) before turning L to descend to Affric Lodge. However, the heather and peaty bogs prevent anything other than walking for the first 2.0 km (1.2 miles). It is better to return to the road along the outward route.

Back at Chisholm Bridge turn R across the bridge and follow the tarmac road SW again for a further 1.84 km (1.14 miles) to the River Affric car park. At the entrance take the middle track of three, the one heading downhill, slightly L of straight on, with one post of the Authorised Vehicles Only on the R and a big rock on the L. Just around the bottom corner cross the river by a bridge, then use the novel bike-slot in the deer-fence gate. Follow the forest road uphill and turn L at the T-junction. This high-quality track provides an easy cycling surface along the edge of the loch.

About 5.2 km (3.2 miles) beyond the bridge there is the first of several deer fences. The gate should not be locked. After a further 2.0 km (1.2 miles) the track divides – take the R fork onto a rougher track. Initially it climbs for 800 metres ending at another gate, the track is then fairly flat for 800 metres, followed by a 1.2 km (0.75 mile) descent.

At the bottom ignore the track that leads out of the forest, fork L to climb once more. There are three 800 metre-long ascents during the next 7.20 km (4.47 miles) section that ends at yet another deer-fence gate. There then follows the short but fast final descent back to the Dog Falls car park.

Places of interest: The Dog Falls and River Affric car parks are start points for a number of waymarked walks of varying lengths.

The bike slot

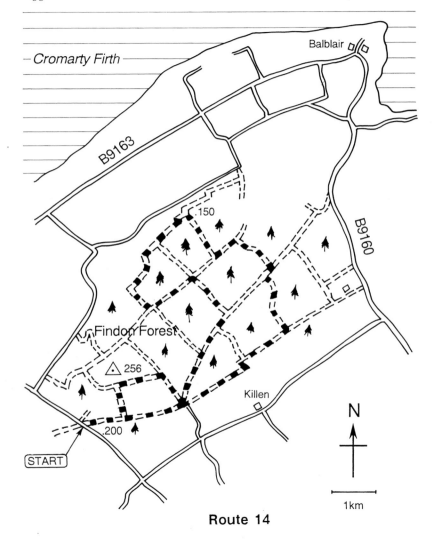

Route 14

14: THE BLACK ISLE

Location/Start & Finish: The Black Isle lies immediately N of the Kessock (Moray Firth) Bridge, Inverness. The Start/Finish is the forestry crossroads at the Mount Eagle transmission mast on the Munlochy to Culbokie road map reference NH 639 578. Do not obstruct the main wide forest entrance, there is room for neatly parked cars in the Old Military Road opposite.

Route: 20 km (12 miles). A circular off-road tour on the very top of the Black Isle. A Forest Enterprise waymarked route for mountain bikes, now also part of the Black Isle Cycle Route. What may look rather uninteresting on the map is enlivened by a variety of surfaces, some excellent views and a fair amount of mud!

Maps: Landrangers 21 Dornoch, Alness & Invergordon area, and 26 Inverness & Loch Ness.

Grading: Moderate 8. Surface 2 and 3, ascent 2, general conditions 1, length 2.

Approaches: From the A9 Tore roundabout at NH 602 524, about 9.6 km (6.0 miles) N of Inverness, take the A832 to Munlochy. In Munlochy turn L just after the garage/petrol station, SP Culbokie. The Mount Eagle mast is 6.4 km (4.0 miles) along this road. You can't miss it! There are no convenient railway stations.

Facilities: Munlochy boasts only the garage, post office, general store, hotel and bar.

Route description: Depart E along the old military road into the forest, SP Learnie, Cromarty and Black Isle Cycle Route. After 960 metres turn L and follow the track gently uphill onto Mount Eagle, 250 m. At the T-junction turn R, then at a second T-junction after a further 1.20 km (0.75 mile) turn R again. Descend this muddy and deeply rutted track, looking to turn L at the bottom, then follow it along the edge of the forest for 1.60 km (0.99 mile).

At the far end turn L then R onto a much firmer forest track. Look to turn L onto the rough track that rises uphill after 1.60 km (1.00 mile). At the end of this one go through the single-bar green gate and turn R. After 300 metres turn L into a track which gently descends for a little over 800 metres. At the next T-junction turn L, then within 800 metres turn R.

At the end of this track there is a junction with a metalled track, turn L and follow it for about 3.20 km (2.00 miles). As the track climbs the hill it becomes rougher, then at the sharp 90 degree turn follow the track around to the L.

At the cross-tracks, turn L rather than continuing uphill, then after 1.2 km (0.70 mile) turn R. At the T-junction at the end, turn R to return to the cross-tracks above Wester Strath, then finally turn R again along the military road to the Finish.

Places of interest: The pretty coastal villages of Fortrose and Rosemarkie are only a few kilometres away from Mount Eagle.

Looking out over the Moray Firth

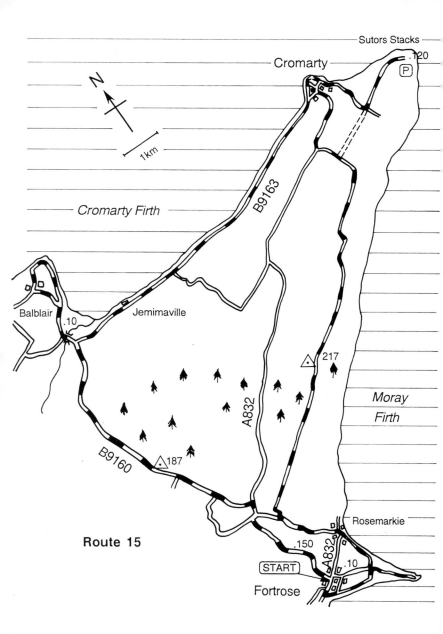

Sutors Stacks

Cromarty

.120

P

N

1km

Cromarty Firth

B9163

Balblair

.10

Jemimaville

△ 217

Moray

Firth

A832

B9160

△187

Rosemarkie

Route 15

.150

A832

.10

START

Fortrose

15: FORTROSE, ROSEMARKIE AND CROMARTY

Location/Start & Finish: The Black Isle, NNE of Inverness on the opposite side of the Moray Firth. Regular Start & Finish point is the cathedral car park on the SE side of the narrow main street in Fortrose, map reference NH 726 565, but a good alternative is Chanonry Point at 749 556, an excellent place to enjoy the view at the end of the ride.

Route: 53 km (33 miles). An on-road circular tour of the eastern end of the Black Isle. The route includes the pretty and historic villages of Fortrose, Rosemarkie and Cromarty. A rural ride dominated by oil rigs!

Map: Landranger 27 Nairn, Forres & surrounding area.

Grading: Moderate 10. Surface 1, ascent 3, general conditions 3, length 3. Primarily quiet roads, three climbs.

Approaches: Fortrose is on the A832, about 11.2 km (7.0 miles) E from the Tore roundabout on the A9. Tore itself is 9.6 km (6.0 miles) N of Inverness. There is no convenient railway station.

Facilities: Fortrose, Rosemarkie and Cromarty each have a few general shops. Cromarty is also well endowed with tea rooms during the summer, but the only one open year round – and limited to weekends only during the winter – is 'The Pantry' on the main street. At the time of writing the town centre pub in Cromarty was up for sale.

Route description: From the cathedral ride ESE through the narrow streets of Fortrose and out through the dunes to Chanonry Point and the lighthouse. Beware of golf balls, wear a helmet! The only return route from the vantage point at the end is back through the dunes.

This time stay on the central road as far as the first narrow junction on the R, SP Golf Club. Turn R and follow this seafront road roughly N to Rosemarkie.

Stay with the seafront until the road becomes the promenade, then turn L up past the museum to A832. Turn R at A832 and follow it over the narrow bridge and steeply uphill for about 1.6 km (1.0 mile) looking to fork R into a minor road, SP Eathie. This narrow road continues to climb for another 3.2 km (2.0 miles).

As the road flattens out along the ridge, giving excellent views of the Moray Firth, eventually it swings sharp L and downhill to the A832 at Newton. At the T-junction turn R at the main road and ride NE to Cromarty, following signs down to the harbour. From the harbour ride past the lighthouse then SE past the football pitch and seafront houses and tearooms, then climb S to Mains Farm. Follow the road as it swings sharply L and out to Sutors Stacks viewpoint. Retrace the rough track back to Cromarty.

Now follow B9163 W along the fringe of Cromarty Bay, with its many rigs, through Jemimaville to B9160. Turn R, then R again after 1.14 km (0.71 mile) out to Newhall Point. Ride round the Point and back inland to Balblair. In the village turn L to rejoin B9163 and follow this road roughly S over the bridge at Newhall Burn, then all the way over the ridge (the road now becoming B9160) past Raddery to A832, a 4.0 km (2.5 mile) ascent, then 3.2 km (2.0 miles) down.

Turn R at A832, then R into a minor road just past the garage after 300 metres, SP Raddery. After a further 200 metres, turn L and climb S over the Hill of Fortrose, 70m of ascent in 800 metres. The descent down the far side offers spectacular views if you stop, but otherwise take care on the corners. In Fortrose turn R along the A832 to the cathedral, or jink L and R to Chanonry Point.

Places of interest: Fortrose Cathedral, Chanonry Point. Cromarty Courthouse Museum, Sutors Stacks with (it is claimed) views over seven counties.

Opposite: A rig in the Sutor Narrows between Cromarty Village and Nigg Ferry

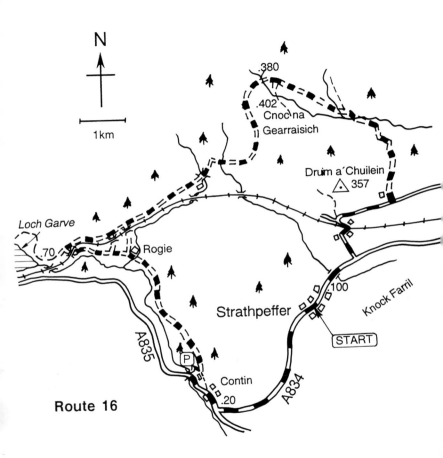

N

1km

.380

.402
Cnoc na
Gearraisich

Druim a´Chuilein
357

Loch Garve

70

Rogie

Strathpeffer

Knock Farril

100

START

A835

A834

P

Contin

.20

Route 16

16: STRATHPEFFER CIRCLE

Location/Start & Finish: Strathpeffer village, 6.4 km (4.0 miles) W of Dingwall, 32 km (20 miles) NW of Inverness. Strathpeffer is on A834 between Dingwall and Contin. Parking in the centre can be congested, the best for our purposes is NE of the shops, near the Eagle Stone turn, signposted on the E side of the road, map reference NH 484 582.

Route: 27 km (17 miles) of which 19.2 km (11.9 miles) is off-road. Rugged upland scenery approached through farmland and plantation forest. After a traverse of exposed upland moor the route follows the Black Water with its pretty waterfalls.

Maps: Landrangers 26 Inverness & Loch Ness, and 20 Beinn Dearg & surrounding area.

Grading: Strenuous 16. Surface 1 – 3, ascent 7, general conditions 4, Length 2. Firm surface. Long initial climb with 320 m of ascent in 6.4 km (4.0 miles).

Approaches: Use A834 from Dingwall; from Inverness follow A9 and A835 to Contin then A834 to Strathpeffer. Dingwall railway station is 6.4 km (4.0 miles) to pick up the route at Heights of Keppoch.

Facilities: Strathpeffer is a spa town with a full range of facilities. Nearby Contin has an hotel, camping and caravan sites. Apart from these there is nothing on the ride route itself.

Route description: Head NE out of Strathpeffer on A834 for about 1.6 km (1.00 mile). After crossing the bridge over the River Peffery turn L into a minor road SP Achterneed. Follow this road as it climbs stiffly up through the hamlet and across the railway line in a series of switchbacks, before eventually heading E high above the valley.

After 2.56 km (1.59 miles) from A834, on the Heights of Keppoch, turn L through a galvanised gate onto a rough tar track, SP Garve 11.5 miles, New House. Keeping to this track, bypass the houses and continue upwards through a scattering of Caledonian pine trees and gorse bushes to a gate which gives access to the forest.

Beyond the gate turn R and follow the forest road uphill. After about 1.6 km (1.0 mile) the track swings sharply L and you get the first views of Ben Wyvis and An Cabar. The track briefly levels out! Just after crossing Abhainn Sgitheach, ignore the track off to the R and continue towards the mountains. There is a further brief climb as the track, which is not marked on the O S map, circles behind Cnoc na Gearraisich.

From the top there is a fast descent over the next 3.2 km (2.0 miles) as some 200m of altitude are lost. Watch out for a couple of sharp bends on the way down. At the bottom there is a plank bridge over a small burn at a ruined croft. After a short climb, and ignoring a further track which rises uphill on the R, there is an 800 metre descent to the rear of Glensgaich. From here it is the hills to the W that dominate the horizon. Although the height above sea level here is less than 150m, the feeling of desolation can be quite acute, especially if the wind is blowing from the W.

Follow the track, which gently descends for 4.8 km (3.0 miles) following the line of the railway and Rogie Burn. Continue past two tracks on the L – short-cuts down to Rogie farm – then take the third turning on the L leading immediately through a small tunnel under the railway. This track then turns SE towards Rogie. Follow the track past the farm and over Rogie Burn. Within 1.6 km (1.0 mile) of the farm it is worth the short detour on the R (signposted) to view Rogie Falls.

Return to the main track and continue SSE for a further 2.4 km (1.5 miles). The track then ends with a 1.12 km (0.70 mile) switchback descent to the Forest Enterprise car park at Contin. At the bottom turn

L past the wooden workshop buildings, then L again at A835 into Contin. At the major junction in the village turn L uphill SP Strathpeffer. From here it is a gentle 3.2 km (2.0 miles) ascent back to the edge of Strathpeffer and a final descent through the village to finish.

Places of interest: Strathpeffer has a museum of childhood, a craft centre, waymarked forest trails and the Touchstone Maze in Blackmuir Wood, at the W end of the village.

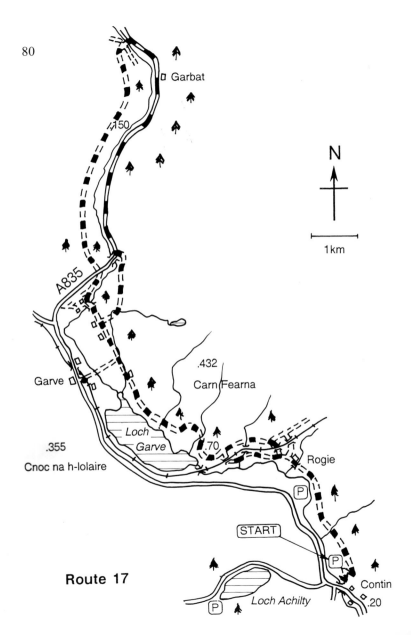

N

1km

Garbat

.150

A835

Garve

.432

Carn Fearna

Loch Garve

.355

Cnoc na h-Iolaire

.70

Rogie

P

START

P

Contin

.20

P

Loch Achilty

Route 17

17: BLACKWATER AND LOCH GARVE

Location/Start & Finish: Contin village, 32 km (20 miles) NW of Inverness, 12.8 km (8.0 miles) W of Dingwall. Start & Finish is the Forestry Enterprise car park 400 metres N of Contin, SP Torrachilty Forest, map reference NH 451 571.

Route: 35 km (22 miles) of which 29.18 km (18.13 miles) is off-road. The route runs through scenic, mixed-age plantation forest before emerging into native birch woodland. It passes Loch Garve and two noted waterfalls on the Black Water. There are excellent views, particularly of Ben Wyvis. The return journey is primarily along the same route.

Maps: Landrangers 26 Inverness & Loch Ness, and 20 Beinn Dearg.

Grading: Energetic 14. Surface 2 – 4, ascent 4, general conditions 1 – 3, length 3. The surfaces are generally firm although it can be muddy in the wooded section. Two streams to ford, although neither too deep!

Approaches: Use A834 from Dingwall, then turn R onto A835 at Contin. From Inverness follow A9 to Tore roundabout, then A835 to Contin. Garve railway station is only 0.94 km (0.58 mile) to pick up the route by Strathgarve Lodge.

Facilities: There is a general store, filling station, hotel, caravan and campsite at Contin, and several B & B establishments in the surrounding area.

Route description: From the car park head back along the entrance drive to the storage sheds (100 metres) and turn L up the forest road SP Garve, Strathpeffer. The road quickly rises 70m through two switchbacks. It then straightens out and heads NNW with a gentle descent. Ignore the tracks heading off to the R.

Within 3.2 km (2.0 miles) of leaving the car park take the path SP Rogie Falls for a worthwhile 400 metre detour, then return to the forest road. Continue roughly N staying with this track as it emerges from the forest, past Rogie farm, and keep the river on your L. Take the tunnel under the railway, then immediately fork L and follow this roughly W with the railway. The stream is usually easy to ford.

The track now narrows as it passes through native birch woodland and swings NW around the shore of Loch Garve. The reflections can be impressive. Watch out for the second stream, it can be deeper than it looks! An easier foot crossing is possible 30 metres downstream.

The track widens again just before Strathgarve Lodge. Cross the very muddy yard in front of the barn and pass under the Lodge on the track beside open pasture. There is now tar seal for 1.6 km (1.0 mile). Continue NNW past Home Farm and the lodge to the bridge over the Black Water where you turn R through Little Garve picnic site and up to A835.

Cross the road and WALK NE for 100 metres to the forest track on the L. The impressive gate will probably be locked but there is a small gate on the R affording access. There is an ascent of 40m as the track rises through the larch trees and then emerges to provide magnificent views firstly of Little Wyvis and then the nose of An Cabar and the Ben Wyvis plateau.

The track flattens out, then gently rises a further 50m up the side of the glen. This section is new and not on the O S map. After about 5.6 km (3.5 miles) there is a sharp descent to a bridge over the river.

From this point you can either retrace your route through the forest or return along the A835. In either event do not go back through the Little Garve picnic site but take the forest track that leads off the A835 just N of the new A835 road bridge over the Black Water, at the wooden SP Little Garve, Garve, Contin. There is a new picnic site and toilets at the SW side of the bridge and a great view of the falls from either structure.

This forest road comes out at Home Farm, then rather than returning through the tunnel, go straight on for about 2.4 km (1.5 miles) and take the track on the R. After 500 metres there is a level crossing and a descent to Rogie farm, where you turn L to rejoin the outward route again to return to Contin.

Places of interest: There are waymarked walks from the 'Start' car park, also W of the A835 at Loch Achilty, and Glen Ord distillery in Muir of Ord has daily guided tours.

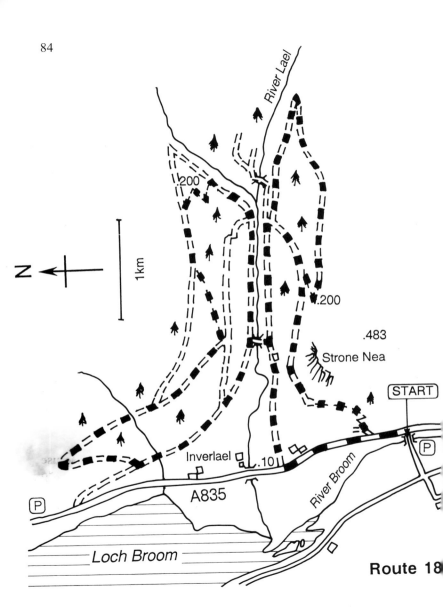

River Lael

N

1km

.200

.200

.483
Strone Nea

START

P

Inverlael

.10

River Broom

A835

P

Loch Broom

Route 18

18: INVERLAEL FOREST

Location/Start & Finish: Inverlael, at the very head of Loch Broom, 11.2 km (7.0 miles) SE of Ullapool on the A835. Start either from the bus shelter at the tiny crossroads near Inverbroom Lodge, map reference NH 181 840 or right next to the A835 at the telephone box where the route rejoins the main road, map reference 181 852, and do the main road bit first.

Route: 16 km (10 miles). An off-road circular tour through the forests of Gleann na Sguaib. The route combines two Forest Enterprise waymarked cycle paths and is primarily on forest tracks, although it does include four more technical sections. There are spectacular views along Loch Broom to the distant Summer Isles and up the glen to Beinn Dearg.

Map: Landranger 20 Beinn Dearg & surrounding area.

Grading: Moderate 10. Surface 2 – 4, ascent 4, general conditions 1, length 1.

Approaches: A835 is the Ullapool to Tore roundabout road; the starting point is 48 km (30 miles) NW of Contin. There is no convenient rail link.

Facilities: There are occasional hotels on A835, otherwise use Ullapool, which is well geared to visitors and an interesting place to visit.

Route description: From the bus shelter return to A835, turn L and head NNW for 400 metres. Turn R onto the tar track, go through the gate in the deer fence, then within 100 metres, and before reaching the end of the track, turn R onto the initially indistinct path that runs through the gorse bushes. The path widens as it rises uphill, but some sections can be very wet and almost unrideable!

As the path nears an area of larch trees, it becomes more solid and widens into a proper track. Follow this into the forest. It eventually turns E and descends to the river. Just before reaching the major T-junction, turn R onto a track that rises gently back uphill. Follow this track up the glen.

After almost 1.5 km (0.9 mile) the track turns sharply back on itself, then after a further 1.2 km (0.75 mile) there is another deer fence and gate. At the end of the track a rough path descends through younger trees, widening as it plunges downhill. By the time it rejoins the main track it resembles a grassy path. Turn R and follow the main track back to the earlier junction.

Turn L at the main junction and follow the River Lael W for 1.2 km (0.75 mile). Turn R across the bridge, then R again to head E. After almost 1.6 km (1.0 mile) the track divides, but go straight on, effectively forking R. After a climb of no more than 500 metres, turn L onto the narrow path that zigzags up the side of the glen. This section is very steep and virtually unrideable.

After 500 metres turn L when the path joins a further track. After about 1.2 km (0.75 mile) turn L again onto a grassy ride which descends across the glen side. At the bottom turn R and climb once more. Follow this track through the deer fence and out onto open moorland.

About 800 metres after leaving the forest, follow the track as it turns sharply L. There is now a 2 km (1.2 miles) descent back to the bridge across the river. Cross the bridge, turn R and return to the A835. Turn L at the main road, it is 1.7 km (1.0 mile) back to the bus shelter.

Places of interest: Lael Forest Garden has a variety of waymarked paths through the Victorian collection of exotic and native tree species. Various car parks along A835 give access. There are also walks through nearby Corrieshalloch Gorge, and around the viewpoint at the Falls of Measach.Both of these can be found a few kilometres south-east of Inverlael

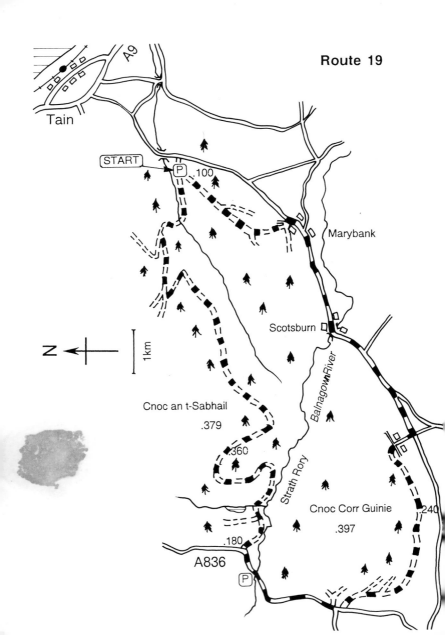

Route 19

19: ALDIE WATER AND STRATH RORY

Location/Start & Finish: Glen Aldie and Strath Rory SW of Tain, N of the Cromarty Firth and about 40 km (25 miles) NNE of Inverness. Start & Finish at the new official forest car park Aldie Burn, map reference NH 757 793.

Route: 34 km (21 miles) of which 25.6 km (15.91 miles) is off-road. A circular tour. A gentle ride through lowland forest is followed by a long ascent across open upland moorland. The return journey incorporates two further but less arduous ascents. There are two fast descents. The route can be muddy in parts.

Map: Landranger 21 Dornoch, Alness & Invergordon area.

Grading: Energetic 15. Surface 3, ascent 5, general conditions 4, length 3.

Approaches: From the A9 N (Dornoch Bridge) take the minor road SP Scotsburn from the Tain bypass. The car park SP Forestry Commission, Aldie Burn is on the R after 2.96 km (1.84 miles). From the A9 S (Cromarty Firth) take the Tomich road SP Scotsburn about 4.8 km (3.0 miles) ENE of Alness. In Badachonacher turn R. The forestry car park is then on the L after 9.8 km (6.1 miles). Tain railway station is 4.25 km (2.64 miles) from the Start car park.

Facilities: Tain has all the facilities one would expect to find in a small town. There is also a camping/caravan site at Meikle Ferry Inn, at the S end of the Dornoch Firth Bridge.

Route description: Turn L out of the car park onto the forest road, then straight on SP Morangie after the electricity lines. Follow the wandering road down over the burn, up to a hairpin L, then WSW for 1.71 km (1.06 miles) to a junction with Footpath crossings. Fork R with the main forest road SP Edderton, where there is also a forest waymarker with purple and green rings.

After 0.52 km (0.32 mile) keep L at another junction – purple and green marker post – then W into an open area culminating at a cross-roads after 1.38 km (0.86 mile). Here turn sharp L, downhill to the burn. Purple only post this time.

Now there is a gentle but steady climb of about 6.4 km (4.0 miles), gaining about 200m. The track heads SE then SW. Within 1.6 km (1.0 mile) of the river crossing you emerge from the trees and there is a gate which gives access to the open moorland. There are almost 360 degree views. Progress is slowed by the soft sandy surface which can feel like a soggy sponge. The track climbs across Cnoc an Dubh Chathair and through a second gate to the saddle above Gleann an Oba. From here there is a fast 2.4 km (1.5 mile) descent into Strath Rory.

At the bottom, cross the burn by the wooden bridge and weave your way W, then NW up to the A836. Turn L onto the main road and follow SW then S for 3.2 km (2.0 miles). Then, about 200 metres after passing the minor road to Ardross, turn L into the track which rises through a farm gate and then a deer fence.

This grassy ride swings slowly E and then runs parallel with Loch Achnacloich. After 3.2 km (2.0 miles) there is a sharp descent to the tar road, but watch out for the gate about 1.6 km (1.0 mile) into the down-hill – it should be possible to steer around it to the R if necessary. At the T-junction turn L then almost immediately R down through the farm buildings at Inchindown.

At the minor road turn L then merge L again after 1.6 km (1.0 mile) to ride through Scotsburn to Marybank. About 150 metres beyond the telephone box, turn L onto the track into the forest – purple bike route marker and green 93 Lamington post. After about 1.5 km (0.93 mile) the track turns very sharply R and climbs gently for another 1.5 km

(0.93 mile). This is another new track and is not on the O S map. It then descends towards the car park. Finally turn R back under the electricity lines to finish.

Places of interest: There are signposted walks from the forest car park.

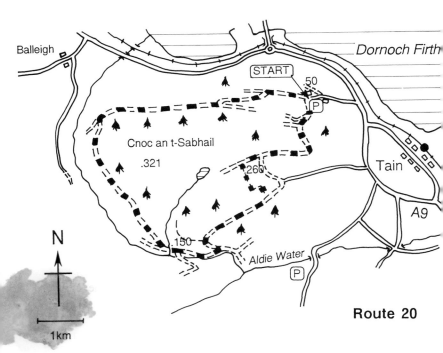

Balleigh

Dornoch Firth

START

50

P

Cnoc an t-Sabhail

.321

.260

Tain

A9

150

Aldie Water

P

N

Route 20

1km

20: MORANGIE FOREST

Location/Start & Finish: Tain, Easter Ross, 56 km (35 miles) NNE of Inverness. Start at forest access gate in Tarlogie village, map reference NH 758 832, marked by a green post bearing 90 Tarlogie. Space for two neatly parked cars.

Route: 18.0 km (11.2 miles) all off road. A circular tour through woodland and forest. Generally low level on tracks which circle Cnoc an t-Sabhail and across Quarryhill. The route offers good views of the coast and hills. There are two short, technical descents.

Map: Landranger 21 Dornoch, Alness & Invergordon.

Grading: Moderate 10. Surface 2, ascent 3, general conditions 2 & 3, length 2.

Approaches: From the A9 at Morangie, just N of Tain, turn W onto the minor road SP Tarlogie. After 800 metres, follow the road into the village, when it turns sharply L & R. The road ends at the forest access gate. The start is 3.2 km (2.0 miles) from Tain railway station.

Facilities: Tain is a small town with all the usual facilities you might expect. There is a camping/caravanning site at the S end of the Dornoch Firth Bridge, at Meikle Ferry Inn.

Route Description: Just inside the forest gate, turn L and climb the forest road through Tarlogie Wood. Where the track divides take the L fork, then at the cross-tracks go straight on. The ascent continues for 2.56 km (1.59 miles). The track then turns sharply to the R.

Follow it as it climbs for almost 1.5 km (0.9 miles). As the track passes under the electricity conductors, turn L up the steep and rough path which follows the lines. This provides a short but technical ascent onto Quarryhill. Continue straight on from the summit the far side of the hill down, roughly following the line of the electricity wayleave. At the junction with the forest road turn R.

After 1.6 km (1.0 mile) there is a sharp bend, followed by a short descent to a T-junction where you turn L. This track divides after about 1.2 km (0.75 mile). Take the R fork' The track then climbs gently for about 1.5 km (0.9 mile).

Continue on this track as it circles the hill for a further 4.8 km (3.0 miles), then as the track emerges into a harvested area above the Dornoch Firth Bridge, turn L onto the rough path which descends in a straight line across the hillside. At the bottom, turn R onto the forest track and return to the entrance gate.

Places of interest: Tain has a local museum and there is the ruined twelfth century St. Duthus' Chapel to visit.

The huge memorial stone to Sir Walter Scott, 'Wizard of the North', though here, opposite the Morangie Distillery, he is some distance north of Abbotsford.

96

21: DORNOCH AND LOCH BUIDHE

Location/Start & Finish: Dornoch, Sutherland, 72 km (45 miles) NNE of Inverness. Start in Dornoch town centre where there is free car parking, map reference NH 799 896.

Route: 42 km (26 miles) of which 8 km (5 miles) off road. A circular tour comprising coastal plain, rural farmland and two river valleys with a remote feel. These are connected via an off-road track through a low pass.

Map: Landranger 21 Dornoch, Alness & Invergordon area. (ROUTE MAP ON PAGES 98 & 99)

Grading: Energetic 10. Surface 1 & 2, ascent 3, general conditions 2, length 3.

Approaches: Dornoch is at the eastern end of the A949, 3.2 km (2.0 miles) E of the A9 trunk road connecting Perth and Wick. Nearest railway station to Dornoch is Tain, some 12.8 km (8.0 miles) distant, but the route could be joined at the Mound on Loch Fleet, which is 6.9 km (4.3 miles) from Golspie station.

Facilities: Dornoch is a very attractive small town geared for visitors with a full range of accommodation. There is a range of shops, several tearooms, hotels and a petrol-filling station on the A9 near the junction with A949

Route description: From the central T-junction near the Dornoch Inn, head WNW for 3.2 km (2.0 miles) to A9. Turn R along the trunk road for 350 metres, then L into a narrow single-track road SP Astle. At the T-junction after 2.86 km (1.78 miles), turn R SP Rearquhar.

This road follows the River Evilix for 4.8 km (3.0 miles). At Achvaich the tar seal ends, but carry on along the valley track. After 1.6 km (1.0 mile), and about 150 metres before Achormlarie, turn R onto the track which passes through a a gate and then climbs the hillside. The ascent is not very arduous but is continuous for nearly 2.4 km (1.5 miles). Vertical ascent is about 140 metres.

At the top the track flattens out and undulates through the pass for 2.4 km (1.5 miles) to Loch Buidhe where you turn R onto the tar road. The final gate has an awkward arrangement at the side. Follow the shore of the loch for 800 metres, then E down Strath Carnaig for nearly 12 km (7.5 miles) to The Mound. Mostly downhill.

Towards the end, the road leaves the wild open moorland to enter dense alder and birch woods which crowd the river's edge. At the T-junction with the A9 turn R, SP Inverness, for 800 metres, then L into the minor road SP Embo. The ruins of Skelbo Castle are on the R after 3.2 km (2.0 miles). The mud flats of Loch Fleet are a noted bird and wildlife sanctuary. Watch out for twitchers' cars.

Ride on past the castle for 960 metres and turn R at the telephone box. Climb 800 metres to the crossroads and turn L. At the T-junction beside Fourpenny, turn R. There are excellent coastal views on this 5.6 km (3.5 miles) section back to Dornoch.

Places of interest: Dornoch has a 13th c. cathedral, a 16th c. Bishop's Palace, good beaches and a renowned golf course. Skelbo Wood, 5 km (3.0 miles) NNW of Dornoch on A9, has a picnic area and waymarked walks.

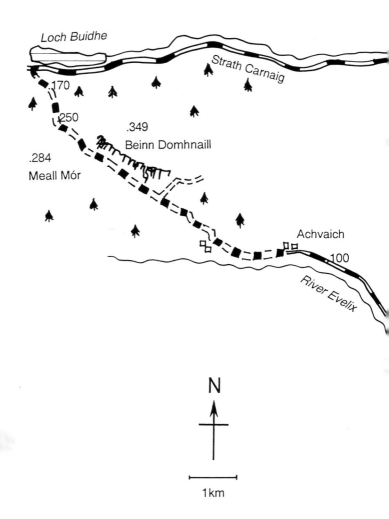

Loch Buidhe

Strath Carnaig

.170

.250

.349
Beinn Domhnaill

.284
Meall Mór

Achvaich

.100

River Evelix

N

1km

Route

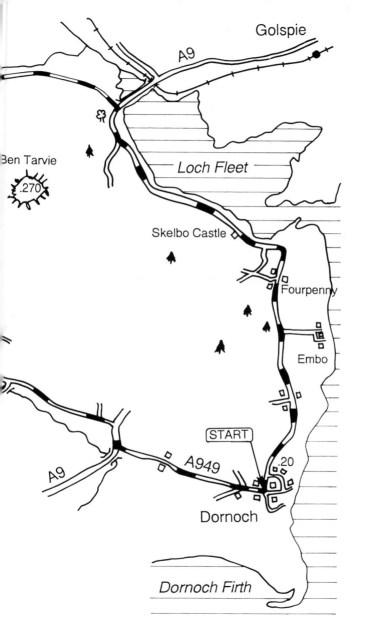

Golspie

A9

Ben Tarvie

.270

Loch Fleet

Skelbo Castle

Fourpenny

Embo

START

A9

A949

.20

Dornoch

Dornoch Firth

LOCHINDORB

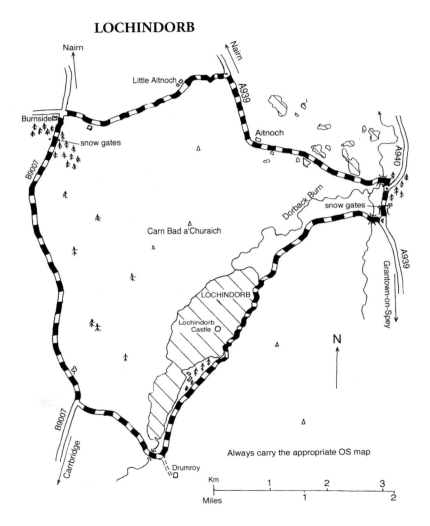

Always carry the appropriate OS map

22: LOCHINDORB

Location/Start & Finish: Lochindorb sits amidst wild bleak country, just W of the A939 between Nairn and Grantown-on-Spey, 32 km (20 miles) ESE of Inverness. Basic start point is the car park afforded by a loop in the old road at NH 976 409 near Little Aitnoch, SP Dunearn, but you may wish to modify this having considered the wind direction on the day!

Route: Circulating around the 1,000 ft. (304.8 m) contour, this 21.95 km (13.64 miles) tarmac circuit embraces some of the bleakest country of the Highlands. There is next to nothing in the way of cover or protection, but on a fine, reasonably still day it is magnificent. On any other day Lochindorb – 'loch of trouble' and home of the Wolf of Badenoch – lives up to its name.

Map: Landranger 27 Nairn & Forres

Grading: Energetic 13. Surface 1, ascent 5, general conditions 5, length 2.

Approaches: From Inverness and Moray district use A96 to Nairn, then SSE on A939 through Ferness to the start. From the S and E aim for Grantown, then N on A939 via Dava. There are no convenient rail stops.

Facilities: Grantown-on-Spey is nearest in a southerly direction, Nairn and Forres to the N. Nothing whatsoever on the route!

Route description: From the lay-by near Little Aitnoch, head SSE onto the A939, over the crest, past Aitnoch and several high level lochans for 4.09 km (2.54 miles), mainly downhill to the tight Bridge of Dava over the Dorback Burn.

Give Way at the junction with the traditional AA box and head S, still with the A939 for 600 metres (0.37 mile) looking to turn R immediately after the bridge beyond the snow gates, SP Lochindorb. Gravel descent to the lower junction, then big undulations for 8.44 km (5.24 miles) to B9007, although the flat winding stretch against the shore at the northern end is good fun.

Turn R down through the dip at the B9007 and head N past the Welcome to Nairnshire board. Then over the western flanks of Carn Bad a' Churaich, with a real feeling of exposure for 5.57 km (3.46 miles) to the Burnside crossroads, heralded by another set of snow gates in the little wood. Look to turn R at the junction but no SP for us.

The last leg runs ENE for 3.25 km (2.02 miles) through Little Aitnoch on a narrow single-track road, and even provides a little cover from natural woodland and head-high bracken after about a mile. The route ends with a rattle over the cattle grid – care when wet.

Places of interest: The island on which Lochindorb Castle stands is partly man-made. Originally the property of the Comyns of Badenoch it was captured by Edward l in 1303, besieged at one time and used as a prison before becoming the Wolf's lair. A unique vegetable, the Lochindorb kale, apparently a cross between red cabbage and the common turnip was alleged to grow in the shelter of the castle walls.

Opposite: Burnside, currently deserted but still substantial, marking the only crossroads on the ride. Only two miles to go, and even a little protection from the weather.

GLENLIVET – ROUTE 1

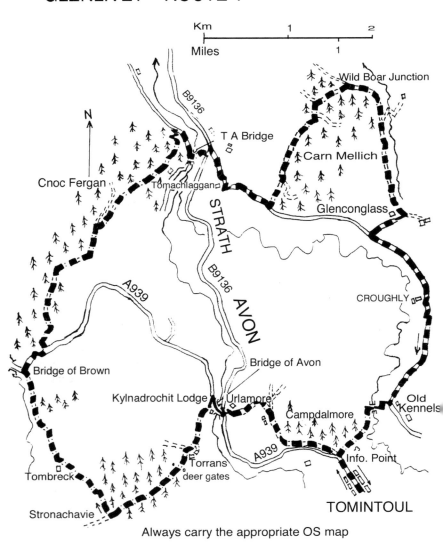

Always carry the appropriate OS map

23: GLENLIVET – ROUTE 1

Location/Start & Finish: Tomintoul, hub of the Glenlivet Estate, is 22 km (13 miles) SE of Grantown-on-Spey, 28 km (18 miles) ENE of Aviemore (as the crow flies) and 58 km (36 miles) by road S of Elgin. The ride starts in the square at Tomintoul, map reference NJ 168 187, but parking is limited. An alternative start can be the Campdalmore information point at NJ 164 194.

Route: 23.46 km (14.48 miles) of which 17.67 km (10.98 miles) is off road on surfaces varying from quad tracks across established pasture to forest roads. Three sections of rutted farm track, one of which is always wet, demand considerable skill. Due to the efforts of the Glenlivet Estate this ride has evolved over the years into a classic Highland route.

Map: Landranger 36 Grantown & Aviemore

Grading: Energetic 14. Surfaces 1 to 5, ascent 6, general conditions 3, length 2.

Approaches: From the S use A9 to Aviemore, then the much improved A95 to Speybridge, and finally A939 to Tomintoul. From Inverness and the N use A9 to Carrbridge, A939, A95, then A939 as above. From Aberdeen, despite its height, use A939 over the Lecht.

Facilities: The Glen Avon hotel in Tomintoul provides substantial meals all year round, otherwise there are seasonal establishments or a trip to Grantown, Carrbridge or Aviemore. Go self-sufficient.

Route description: At the time of writing – September 2003 – the route was due to be waymarked 'Route 1' by the Glenlivet Estate. Depart NNW down the main street of Tomintoul for 0.88 km (0.55 mile) to Campdalmore Information Point lay-by, where the A939 swings L. Fork R, uphill onto a compacted dirt estate road and ride above but parallel to the A939. SP Public Path to Dorback via Bridge of Avon.

Ride around to Campdalmore Farm, where keep L down the old track to the lower gate. Swing L after the first gate, downhill and rutted, straight on at the wicket at Urlarmore Farm, then finally down to a flight of unrideable steps after 1.92 km (1.19 miles).

Urlarmore, Bridge of Avon, B9136. Turn L to A939, T-junction turn R across the new Bridge of Avon, then hairpin L towards Kylnadrochit Lodge, but keep R above the house on the forest road. Scottish Rights of Way Society and Glenlivet way-markers keep you right. Follow the forest road above the Lodge, keep R then L at Torrans, down through the galvanised deer gates and on to the edge of the forest after 1.52 km (0.94 mile).

Stronachavie gate. Turn R steeply uphill, parallel to the wood, SP Bridge of Brown. Grassy to col, 465m, over crest, downhill to gate and L with main track, L again back through fence after 110 metres, then diagonally downhill NW to far end of Tombreck. Bear R at Tombreck, wet and rutted to gate, then rough and stony downhill – big erosion, keep high. Then through the little wood, and follow the obvious but wet track to A939. A little 'G' post guides you R up an impossible hill at far end after 2.43 km (1.51 miles).

Bridge of Brown, A939. Turn R up steep tarmac for 0.42 km (0.26 mile) to forest entrance on L at top of hill. Turn L into wide, gated forest entrance, no SP, fork R in 60 metres, then ride roughly N for 1.98 km (1.23 miles) to internal forest junction. Big dip past quarry. In Cnoc Fergan wood turn R and immediately L onto a newer forest road and ride NNE for 1.80 km (1.12 miles) to tarmac in Strath Avon.

Strath Avon. Steep downhill approach to T-junction. Turn R with narrow tarmac road, downhill past cottage to Territorial Army suspension bridge on L after 410 metres. 'G' marker, little gate onto bridge, planks run the 'wrong' way' – walk across! Turn L at far side of bridge, then R up side of field to public road. Aim for the knackered birch tree at the top! All happens in 0.62 km (0.39 mile)!

B9136. 'T-junction' turn L, then hairpin R in 40 metres, SP Croughly. Uphill for 1.34 km (0.83 mile) to forest entrance beyond Tomachlaggan. Clear felling on approach to junction. Turn L onto forest road through Carn Mellich Wood, steady climb. Keep L over crest after 0.41 km (0.25 mile), over col, 396m, swing L downhill with main track after 1.25 km (0.78 mile) then keep R when confronted with deer fence, and downhill to the T-junction after 2.07 km (1.29 miles).

Wild Boar junction. T-junction turn R and follow SSE for 2.10 km (1.30 miles) to Glenconglass, looking to turn R with tarmac after the cattle grid. Swing R uphill, over the little col, 337m, then downhill to the grassy T-junction. Swing L and ride SE through Croughly Farm looking for Speyside Way markers on L then R after 3.23 km (2.01 miles). 100 metres before The Old Kennels turn R over stile with Speyside Way. SP 'Please descend directly to footbridge', but you can't see it! Aim for the bend in the river between the birches. Walk down! Several lifts over fences and onto wooden bridge. Follow Speyside Way posts up onto lip of bank, the L along to fence, which you follow until it becomes a track. Campdalmore Information Point reached after 1.09 km (0.68 miles).

Information Point lay-by. Turn L onto A939 and back into Tomintoul.

Places of interest: (Who needs more after all this excitement?)

TOMNAVOULIN

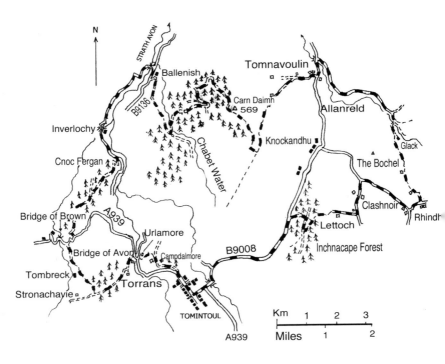

Always carry the appropriate OS map

24: TOMNAVOULIN

Location/Start & Finish: Tomintoul , administrative centre of the Glenlivet Estate is 22 km (13 miles) SE of Grantown-on-Spey and 28 km (18 miles) ENE of Aviemore (as the crow flies). Nominally the ride starts in the square at Tomintoul, map reference NJ 168 188, where there is limited street parking, but an official car park is only 100 metres away in the street parallel to, but W of the A939.

Route: 51.78 km (32.16 miles) of which 31.29 km (19.44 miles) is off-road on just about every surface you can imagine, from pristine forest roads to the faintest tracks across pasture, and including a monumental rutted stony downhill off Carn Daimh (pronounced Die!), the highest point on the route, 569 m.

Map: Landranger 36 Grantown & Aviemore.

Grading: Strenuous 18. Surfaces 1 to 5, ascent 7, general conditions 4, length 4.

Approaches: From the S, use A9 to just N of Aviemore, then the much improved A95 to Speybridge, and finally A939 to Tomintoul. From Inverness and the N use A9 to Carrbridge, A939, A95, then A939 to Tomintoul. From Aberdeen consider using A939 over the Lecht. There is no convenient railway.

Facilities: Year-round eateries are limited to the Glen Avon Hotel in Tomintoul and the Pole Inn, Knockandhu, map ref. NJ 213 237 which is open most days. Best plan is self-sufficiency!

Route description: Depart NNW from Tomintoul on A939 for 0.88 km (0.55 mile) to Campdalmore Information Point lay-by, where the

A939 swings L. Fork R uphill onto a good compacted dirt road and ride above but parallel to the A939. SP Public Path to Dorback via Bridge of Avon.

Follow to Campdalmore Farm, where keep L down the old track to the lower gate. Swing L after the first gate, downhill and rutted, straight on through the wicket at Urlarmore farm, then finally down a flight of unrideable steps to the B9136 after 1.92 km (1.19 miles).

Urlarmore, Bridge of Avon, B9136. Turn L to A939, T-junction turn R across new Bridge of Avon, then hairpin L towards Kylnadrochit Lodge in 100 metres, but keep R above the house on the forest road. Scottish Rights of Way Society and Glenlivet way-markers keep you right. Follow the forest road above the Lodge, keep R then L at Torrans, down through the galvanised deer gates and around to the forest edge after 1.52 km (0.94 mile).

Stronachavie gate. Turn R steeply uphill, parallel to the wood, SP Bridge of Brown. Grassy to col, 465m, over crest, downhill to gate and L with main track, L again back through fence after 110 metres, then diagonally downhill NW above Tombreck. Bear R just beyond Tombreck, wet and rutted to gate, then rough and stony downhill – big erosion, keep high. Then through the little wood, and follow obvious but wet track to A939. A little 'G' post guides you up an impossible hill at the far end to A939 after 2.43 km (1.51 miles).

Bridge of Brown, A939. Turn R up steep tarmac for 0.42 km (0.26 mile) to forest entrance at top of hill. Turn L into wide, gated forest entrance, no SP, then fork R in 60 metres and ride roughly N for 1.98 km (1.23 miles) to internal forest junction. Big dip past quarry. In Cnoc Fergan wood turn R and immediately L onto a newer forest road and ride NNE for 1.80 km (1.12 miles) to tarmac in Strath Avon.

Fast downhill approach to public road in Strath Avon where T-junction turn L and follow through Inverlochy for 4.48 km (2.78 miles) to wood-decked bridge and B9136. T-junction turn R at the post box, onto B9136 for 200 metres, then fork L uphill past Ballenlish. 'G' markers guide you into the stony track, around the hairpin and through the gate onto an old stony road. Stick with the main track up through the woods and eventually L out onto open pasture at a gate by a hut. After a total of 2.98 km (1.85 miles) look to turn L about 400 metres after re-entering forestry.

Main forest junction. Turn L down over Chabet Water and climb around Tom a' Chor for 2.01 km (1.25 miles) to the head of the glen. Then turn L over the burn beneath the quarry, fork R within 80 metres and look to fork R onto a lesser forest road after a further 0.58 km (0.36 miles). 'G' markers should keep you right again. Then follows the final, often damp, 2.19 km (1.36 miles) climb to the summit of Carn Daimh.

Carn Daimh, 569m. Stile, then straight over the top onto stony downhill twin-track. Soft through woods, lumpy down to junction after 2.11 km (1.31 miles). T-junction turn L, huge SP Tomnavoulin. Soft, wet, rutted, then grassy fields and farm tarmac for further 4.49 km (2.79 miles) to Tomnavoulin.

Tomnavoulin. T-junction turn L at B9008, then look to turn R after 0.72 km (0.45 mile) after the old bridge SP Tombae, into Glenlivet. Ride roughly SE for 3.94 km (2.45 miles) to end of tarmac at Allanreid car park. Bear R across bridge with green barriers, onto unsealed road towards Achdregnie. Follow 'G' markers across to footbridge after 270 metres and cross River Livet towards Glack. About 200 metres before Glack turn R at 'G' marker and follow soft track/sheep trod diagonally to high level gate above Glack after 1.31 km (0.81 miles). 'Tracks' merge at gate, then contour around The Bochel on 'technical' single track, roughly S to Rhindhu. Soft in places. Turn R (WSW) at Rhindhu to T-junction at Chapeltown, then R again towards Knockandhu looking to turn hairpin L, uphill when the 'main' road bears R after 5.25 km (3.26 miles), SP Clashnoir Experimental Farm.

Ride S over the crest, down past Clashnoir to the Lettoch turn at a bus shelter after 1.27 km (0.79 miles). Follow ancient Right of Way past Lettoch, through the conglomeration, then bear L and R when the very stony tractor track ends on the edge of the moor. Then over the col on an even rougher track to the forest, reached after 1.51 km (0.94 mile). Straight into Inchnacape Forest on soft, wet track which gradually improves, then after 0.90 km (0.56 mile) turn R at a forest crossroads, downhill through bends and L in 0.64 km (0.40 mile) through clear-felled area to the main road.

B9008, T-junction turn L past the peat workings and mainly SW for 5.26 km (3.27 miles) all the way to Tomintoul.

Places of interest: Join the 'Whisky Trail'!

on the W side of the Corrieyairack Pass. We were assured that the riderless horse was a spare.

ember morning in the Spey valley near Laggan.

Crossing the Allt Chomhraig, Inshriach Forest. It was rideable on the day. (Route 2)

Allt Mor crossing. Sorting out the best route, but still wet up to the knees.

azard en route to Loch Gamhna. The tree doesn't look that big until you compare it with the ike. (Route 3)
urma Road: the last two trees at ca. 500 m.

Tea beside Loch Morlich: The Cairngorms in the background.

Emma Guy and Paul Eynon bound for the head of Loch Affric (coast to coast crossing).

Watch out for wet tree roots. Scots pine have extensive, tough and slippery anchors. Treat them with great respect. This specimen is in Glen More.

Nr Dalcrombie, above Loch Ruthven; the high point on route 9. Cliffs of Creag nan Clach behir

Remnants of the old ford at Banchor Bridge. Note the unusual but effective paving method.

e right way to ride. Along the seafront at Rosemarkie.

hanonry Point, Fortrose, on the Black Isle.

Afternoon sun lighting a track leading from the Torrachilty Forest carpark (Route 17).

Little Garve Farm, the hub of route 17. The bridge over the Black Water can just be seen.

Looking across Loch Oich from a high-level section of the Great Glen Cycle Route – a ride of great contrast.

The TA footbridge in Strath Avon, Glen Livet Estate. Note how the planks of the main deck suddenly lie the 'wrong' way for bikes – you have been warned.

Rounding the shoulder of Letterach, Glen Livet Estate, on stony but rideable twin track.

Heading N from Loch Linnhe on the wide, well-surfaced canal towpath near Banavie.

Brunachan Croft, Glen Roy, backed by low-level Parallel Roads.

The most luxurious place in the book – upstairs in Luib-chonnal bothy.

In Glenconglass: The lads nearly fell off their bikes when they saw the family of wild boar (in the field to the right).

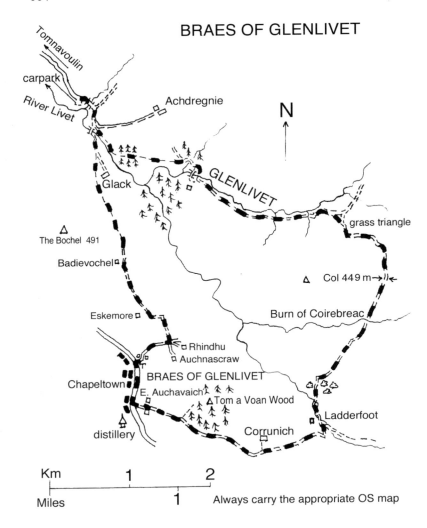

BRAES OF GLENLIVET

Tomnavoulin
carpark
River Livet
Achdregnie
N
GLENLIVET
Glack
grass triangle
△ The Bochel 491
Badievochel □
△ Col 449 m →)|←
Eskemore □
Burn of Coirebreac
□ Rhindhu
Auchnascraw
BRAES OF GLENLIVET
Chapeltown
E. Auchavaich △ Tom a Voan Wood
Ladderfoot
Corrunich
distillery

Km   1   2
Miles   1   Always carry the appropriate OS map

25: BRAES OF GLENLIVET

Location/Start & Finish: Glenlivet, western flanks of the Ladder Hills, Moray. Start from the Allanreid car park, mid Glenlivet, map reference NJ 236 248.

Route: 15.55 km (9.66 miles) all of which, except 0.93 km (0.58 mile) is off-road. A brilliant circular tour embracing just about every surface you can imagine, through Glenlivet and up onto the flanks of Carn na Glascoill, returning through 'The Braes'. Many fords!

Maps: Landrangers 36 Grantown & Aviemore, and 37 Strathdon, but the entire route is covered by Explorer (1:25,000) 420 Correen Hills & Glenlivet.

Grading: Energetic 15. Surface 2, 3, 4 and 5, ascent 7, general conditions 4, length 1.

Approaches: Aim for Tomnavoulin, 58 km (36 miles), as the crow flies, ESE of Inverness, 77 km (48 miles) WNW of Aberdeen, and 35 km (22 miles) NE of Aviemore, on the B9008 between Tomintoul and Dufftown. The final turn is 600 metres N of the centre (the shop!) of Tomnavoulin, immediately N of the old bridge, SP Tombae. Then follow this twisty single track road all the way to Allanreid car park at the very end of the tarmac. You will find a neat SP and information board on the R when you arrive.

Facilities: There is nothing at all in the way of refreshment on the route, despite the fact you pass the immaculate Knockandhu distillery! The Pole Inn, on the B9008 at Knockandhu, does food and B & B, thereafter Tomintoul is only real alternative.

Route description: Turn R away from the Allanreid car park, Glenlivet, swing R over the bridge with green barriers, then straight on into the Achdregnie road, past the innovative half-tyre flower basket! Glenlivet Walk 3 markers.

After 270 metres fork R onto the grass at the tiny 'G' marker post and aim for the bridge. Do not cross the bridge, save that for the return leg, but keep to the wide grass track that hugs the N side of the River Livet until you reach a gate into woods after 0.97 km (0.60 mile).

Ride E through the woods on well-defined but lumpy twin-track, then when the track disappears as you reach pasture follow the blue 'G' markers along the fence, with the power lines. The twin-track reappears at the far side of the pasture, then aim for the distant footbridge opposite the lonely cottage after 1.03 km (0.64 mile).

This crossing of the Livet has both bridge and ford, but the ford is not as smooth as the last one! Use the bridge, then bear L below the cottage to the gate, where the track improves to a good gritty surface. Ride roughly SE up Glenlivet for 1.82 km (1.13 miles) to a gate/stile, with the river and fence on your L. There is yet another ford just before the gate.

Gate at bend. This is where we lose the 'Walk 3' markers – the pedestrians turn R up the fence. Continue roughly ENE with the twin-track (the sheep having provided a smoother option up the middle!) for 310 metres, when you fork R at a noticeably green area of a huge grass triangle. We want to swing R up the hill, but disregard the tempting 6WD tracks off to the R about 60 metres earlier, they are unrideable. Turn R again at the far side of the triangle then look to weave L and R up the main track and around to the hidden col on the flanks of Carn na Glascoill. This is a stiff, gritty climb interspersed with sizeable lumps of marble before you reach the col after 1.59 km (0.99 mile).

The col, apart from obviously being 'the top' is marked by a large turning area, then it is straight downhill to the little lumpy ford at the Burn of Coirebreac, the track becoming rough at the steepest part! There is a bit of a climb beyond the ford, which comes as a surprise because it all looks like a downhill from the top, then around to a gate at the juniper bushes after 1.70 km (1.06 miles).

Follow the obvious but rutted lumpy track around past Ladderfoot, via a couple of fords of course. Then swing sharply W, down past Corrunich, where you keep L across to the wood (which may be well felled by now!) and a gate which is usually open, after 1.92 km (1.19 miles). Stick with the estate track up past Tom a Voan Wood, then L down the red road through East Auchavaich to the public road at Chapeltown, just N of the immaculate Knockandhu distillery, after a further 1.61 km (1.00 mile).

Turn R through what has got to be the shortest 30 mph zone in Scotland, looking to turn R again after 0.59 km (0.37 mile) SP Footpath to Auchnascraw (The Livet Path) Walk 3. The actuality is that it is a single-track tarmac road as far as the 'crossroads' at Auchnascraw/Rhindhu where you turn L onto a loose downhill farm road. Then wiggle L and R but overall steadily N past Eskemore and Badievochel to skirt the eastern shoulder of The Bochel, which has been in view from the entire route. An adequate number of Glenlivet fingerposts and repeaters keep you right, but so difficult is the single track through the lumpy moorland N of Badievochel, you could be forgiven for questioning the route! However, it only lasts about 300 metres, and thereafter is a joy to ride to the gate above Glack, reached after 3.01 km (1.87 miles).

From the high gate, the final, single-track downhill takes you diagonally across the pasture. Aim for a point about 200 metres N of Glack, using the best sheep track! When you reach the farm road merge L along to the bridge at the River Livet – you can use the ford if you feel brave – then L across the grass and back to Allanreid car park after 1.31 km (0.81 mile).

Places of interest: Tomnavoulin (now Tamnavoulin) Distillery may do tours, and used to have a small café, but at the time of writing the situation was fluid!

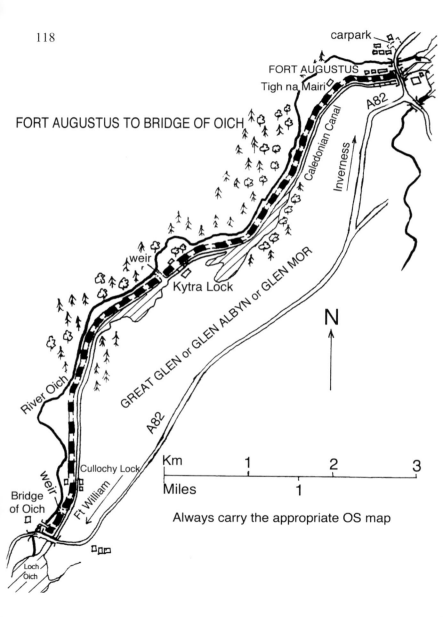

FORT AUGUSTUS TO BRIDGE OF OICH

carpark

FORT AUGUSTUS

Tigh na Mairi

Caledonian Canal

A82

Inverness

weir

Kytra Lock

GREAT GLEN or GLEN ALBYN or GLEN MOR

N

River Oich

A82

Ft William

Km 1 2 3

Miles 1

weir

Cullochy Lock

Bridge of Oich

Always carry the appropriate OS map

Loch Oich

26: FORT AUGUSTUS TO BRIDGE OF OICH

Location/Start & Finish: Fort Augustus sits at the southern end of Loch Ness, 55 km (34 miles) SW of Inverness, 52 km (32 miles) NE of Fort William. The route follows the Caledonian Canal between Loch Ness and Loch Oich. Start & Finish is nominally alongside the locks in Fort Augustus, map reference NH 378 092, the large, well signposted main car park (60p for 10 hours in September 2003) being 100 metres N of the canal at the side of the A82.

Route: Fort Augustus – Bridge of Oich 8.05 km (5.00 miles), 7.43 km (4.62 miles) of which is off-road in the shape of vehicle-width canal towpath, all of which is stony, but flat apart from slight rises at the locks. The 'out-and-back' distance is double!

Map: Landranger 34 Fort Augustus & Glen Albyn area.

Grading: Moderate 6. Surface 2, ascent 1, general conditions 2, length 1. You might expect the 'general conditions' along the canal to be 'low level, sheltered', especially as most of the canal fringe is tree-lined, but by the very nature of the Great Glen, any wind tends to be channelled between the hills which can make one direction hard work, but the other a delight!

Approaches: The main Inverness – Fort William A82 is the only real through route. No rail links.

Facilities: Fort Augustus is well geared to visitors, with B & Bs, hotels, good pub grub at the Lock Inn, toilets and shops. There is virtually nothing at Bridge of Oich apart from the Thistle Stop about a mile NE on the A82, but this main road is to be avoided if at all possible.

Route Description: Depart W from McVean's shop on the N side of the lock in Fort Augustus on narrow tarmac up the one-sided street. The sealed surface ends after 0.62 km (0.39 mile) at the white cottage of Tigh na Mairi and you head SW on well-surfaced but stony canal towpath.

Trees flank the W side of the track for most of the way to Kytra Lock, some 3.46 km (2.15 miles) distant, but if you stop and peer through the trees you will see that you are riding on a strip of elevated land little wider than the track for much of the way. In spate conditions the River Oich can be roaring away on your R, whilst the canal, in comparison, meanders calmly on your L.

Stick with the towpath past Kytra Lock, the prettiest spot on the Caledonian Canal until you reach Cullochy Lock a further 3.29 km (2.04 miles) to the SSW, but soon after passing Kytra you encounter the first weir or spillway, an overflow system for this long stretch. Water seldom runs across the weir, but take due notice before crossing.

The lock keeper at Cullochy is to be complimented on the overall appearance of the place. Pause a minute and have a word or two. Then continue SW for the final 0.68 km (0.42 mile) to Bridge of Oich, with a minor 'sting-in-the-tail' at the rather lumpy weir after 200 metres.

Bridge of Oich is actually the suspension bridge over the River Oich, the large swing-bridge over the canal is called Aberchalder Bridge, and the modern road bridge over the river is called Oich Bridge!

Hopefully you will have the wind at your back for the return journey.

The lock, and an ornamental 'Nessie', Fort Augustus. The ride departs along the right-hand side of the canal, indicated as 'No Through Road'.

CORPACH TO GAIRLOCHY

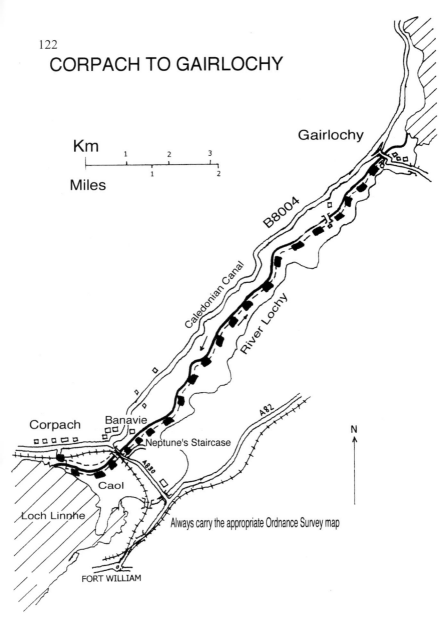

Km

Miles

Gairlochy

B8004

Caledonian Canal

River Lochy

Corpach

Banavie

Neptune's Staircase

Caol

A830

A82

Loch Linnhe

Always carry the appropriate Ordnance Survey map

N

FORT WILLIAM

27: CORPACH TO GAIRLOCHY

Location/Start & Finish: Caledonian Canal near Fort William. Start from the village hall car park, Corpach, space for 40 cars, map reference NN 095 767.

Route: 24.78 km (15.40 miles) of off-road canal towpath between Corpach and Gairlochy. Initially it was hoped that this would have been a figure-of-eight ride, but the plans to utilise the western towpath have not come to fruition. However, watch this space! The return journey can be made along B8004 to Banavie, but this adds a little extra in terms of distance and despite the tarmac surface the hills make it more difficult.

Map: Landranger 41 Ben Nevis, Fort William & Glen Coe.

Grading: Moderate 7. Surface 2, ascent 1 and 2, general conditions 1, length 2. The 'general conditions' can vary greatly. Yes, it is low level, yes, it is flanked by trees along most of its length, but look at the shape of the trees between Corpach and Banavie. If the wind is anywhere between WSW and S it can howl up the Caledonian Canal!

Approaches: Aim for Fort William, then less than a kilometre NE of the town on A82, take A830, SP Mallaig, to Corpach some 3.00 km (1.85 miles) distant, crossing the Caledonian Canal en route. In Corpach turn L at the big SP Caledonian Canal, Car Park, Picnic area, then park at the village hall before crossing the railway. There are railway stations at Corpach and Fort William.

Facilities: There is a pub and shop in Corpach, a hotel at Banavie, but a full range of facilities in Fort William. In the summer months there is a little shop at Neptune's Staircase, but nothing else on the route.

Route description: Turn L out of the car park, down over the level crossing – paying due heed to any signals – then R and immediately L over the lock gates to the seaward side of the Caledonian Canal. 'Cyclists Please Dismount'. There are often interesting craft in the basin.

Ride E then NE in a long curve on the canal towpath past Caol for 2.08 km (1.29 miles) to the railway and road crossing at A830, Banavie. There are lots of signs, most important being 'Stop, Look & Listen' when crossing the railway. If you arrive here about 1035 during the summer months it might be the 'Jacobite' steam train approaching.

Straight on across the A830 at the side of the swing bridge, then NE up the side of Neptune's Staircase SP Great Glen Cycle Route, Gairlochy. There is always something of interest in the locks. Keep to the towpath on the E side of the canal for 6.58 km (4.08 miles). You can't go wrong! There is a single gate soon after you clear the Banavie basin, thereafter your run will be unimpeded.

After 6.58 km (4.08 miles) there is a track off to the R on one of the tighter bends, but a 'Thistle' SP confirms that you stick to the towpath. It is then a further 3.73 km (2.32 miles) to Gairlochy.

The return route can either be back along the towpath, which looks surprisingly different in this direction, especially in the latter stages when you are looking straight down Loch Linnhe for many miles, or along the twisty B8004.

When you reach Banavie you can use the western towpath for the last leg back to Corpach, but the views are better on the Caol side.

The upper basin at the head of Neptune's Staircase, Banavie

GLEN ROY

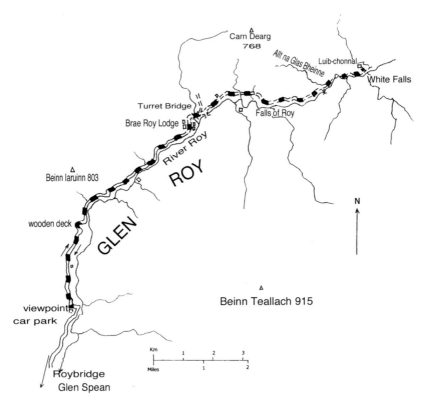

Carn Dearg
768

Allt na Glas Bheinne

Luib-chonnal

White Falls

Turret Bridge

Falls of Roy

Brae Roy Lodge

River Roy

ROY

Beinn Iaruinn 803

GLEN

wooden deck

N

viewpoint
car park

Beinn Teallach 915

Km   1   2   3
Miles   1   2

Roybridge
Glen Spean

Always carry the appropriate Ordnance Survey map

28: GLEN ROY

Location/Start & Finish: Glen Roy, accessed via Glen Spean 24 km (15 miles) NE of Fort William. Start from the Viewpoint car park, 5.5 km (3.4 miles) NNE of Roybridge, map reference NN 297 852. The purely off-road section of the ride can be started from the gates of the Brae Roy Lodge estate, map reference NN 334 911 where there is space for two neatly parked cars.

Route: 33.06 km (20.54 miles) of which 16.72 km (10.39 miles) is off road in the upper reaches of Glen Roy. This is a stunning ride in unique countryside, the 'parallel roads' you see marked on the O S map not being roads at all, but terraces, thought to be the shoreline of a glacial loch at different stages of its life. The latter stages of the section from Brae Roy Lodge to Luib-chonnal is one of the most wildly beautiful places in Great Britain – a subjective view, granted, but not without foundation!

Map: Landranger 34 Fort Augustus & Glen Albyn.

Grading: Strenuous 17. Surface 1, 3 and 5, ascent 6, general conditions 4, length 3.

Approaches: There is only one way into Glen Roy, that is from Roybridge, which is on A86 Spean Bridge to (Dalwhinnie)/Kingussie/Laggan road, 5 km (3 miles) E of the A82/A86 junction at Spean Bridge. Turn NE in Roybridge onto the minor road at the W side of the River Roy, SP Glen Roy, Brae Roy, Village Hall, and additionally 'Road unsuitable for coaches'. (The only people met on the ride were a couple, the lady of which admitted she had demanded her husband turn back on this initial road before he reached the car park! But he couldn't find a turning place, so they continued!) There is a railway station at Roybridge.

Facilities: There are several B & Bs, two hotels and a post office/ shop in Roy Bridge. Nothing on the ride route. Treat it as a wilderness tour!

Route description: Depart roughly N, downhill from the car park and follow the twisty, undulating, single-track Glen Roy road N then NE for a total of 8.17 km (5.08 miles) to the Brae Roy Lodge Estate entrance. 'No Parking Beyond This Point'. Care at the bridge in the U-bend after 3.11 km (1.93 miles) – fast approach but wooden deck; could be slippery when wet. The entrance to the estate can be the alternative start point.

Follow the tarmac through the buildings comprising Brae Roy Lodge for 0.96 km (0.60 mile) to Turret Bridge. Note the barn on the L with the antlers. The road becomes loose well before the bridge. Swing R across the bridge (no option!) then keep R onto the lower track and head ENE then NE hugging the N side of the River Roy for 1.38 km (0.86 mile) to a little bridge in the last of the trees. The ford is loose but smooth!

Continue roughly E from the bridge, the undulations getting bigger after the Falls of Roy. A mostly wide but very stony stalkers road for the next 4.07 km (2.53 miles). Several little fords. The number of 'parallel roads' diminishes. Distant glimpse of bothy in the latter stages. Only tangible markers are the deep fords of Allt na Glas Bheinne opposite a little footbridge over the River Roy.

Stick with the riverside road, which becomes much flatter for the next 1.66 km (1.03 miles) until opposite the White Falls, which in turn are opposite Luib-chonnal bothy. Turn L onto a soft grassy track that carries you across to the front door in 290 metres.

Only when you turn around and start to retrace your route do you realise it is actually very downhill on the way back. Enjoy it but stop occasionally and drink in the view. There are few places to match it.

Luib-chonnal bothy at the head of Glen Roy. In the background, right, is the shallow watershed spawning the headwaters of the River Spey in Corrieyairack Forest. It flows out into the North Sea; on this side of the watershed the River Roy runs out into the Atlantic.

TORR MOR

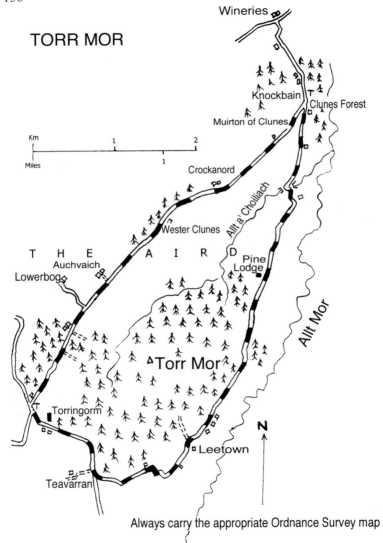

Wineries

Knockbain

Clunes Forest

Muirton of Clunes

Km

1   2

Miles

1

Crockanord

Wester Clunes

Allt a' Choiliach

T   H   E   A   I   R   D   Pine
                                        Lodge

Auchvaich

Lowerbog

Allt Mor

△Torr Mor

N

Torringorm

Leetown

Teavarran

Always carry the appropriate Ordnance Survey map

29: TORR MOR

Location/Start & Finish: The Aird, 13 km (8 miles) W of Inverness. Start from Clunes forest entrance at map reference NH 555425. There us a small car park within the forest, but at the time of writing the gate was locked, despite the fact that Woodland Walks are signposted. Space for two neatly parked cars without obstructing the entrance; also space at the telephone kiosk 50 metres N of the gate.

Route: 12.73 km (7.91 miles) all tarmac. A short but testing circular ride round the hill of Torr Mor with almost all the climbing done on the outward leg and the return finishing with a good downhill. A convenient training run for Inverness. On windy days, a lot more exposed than it looks.

Map: Landranger 26 Inverness & Loch Ness

Grading: Energetic 11. Surface 1, ascent 5, general conditions 4, length 1.

Approaches: On A862 12 km (7.4 miles) W of the Caledonian Canal bridge in Inverness, look for SP Moniak Wineries. Follow this road SE then SW to the winery, then first L uphill, SP Clunes, Great Glen Way, through Knockbain for 1.1 km (0.70 miles) to the forest entrance just beyond the telephone kiosk. Nearest railway stations are Muir of Ord, 13.00 km (8.1 miles) to the NW, and Inverness 16.6 km (10.3 miles) to the E.

Facilities: There is nothing on route but Muir of Ord or Inverness should cater for all your needs.

Route Description: The start is at a pronounced fork in the road S of the Knockbain telephone kiosk. Depart S on the single-track minor road, SP Great Glen Way, past a bungalow on the L. There is also a red on white 'M. Mhor' arrow nailed to the tree in the fork. Initially, the road is fairly level as far as the bridge over the Allta'Choillich, but the hill kicks in as soon as you cross. Navigation is easy over these first 6.15 km (3.82 miles) – you simply follow the tarmac round the SE side of Torr Mor, but this part of the ride is a relentless climb, biting hard about Pine Lodge (but that could have been me running out of puff).

As you crest the hill the Scots Pine seem to look particularly wind-swept, verging on the battered. After you pass the house with no name, it's gently downhill for a little way, then gently uphill again perched on the hillside above the Allt Mor towards Leetown – aptly named when the wind is in the W. In that case, expect a buffeting as you round the southern shoulder of the hill to the junction at Teavarran.

Teavarran hosts the Moniack Mhor Writers' Centre and the junction affords impressive views to N, S, SE & W, the snow-trimmed peaks of Ben Wyvis decorating the skyline on the day the route was checked.

Now swing R, straight on past the road on the L at Teavarran and downhill for 1.30 km (0.81 mile) to the kiosk junction near Torringorm, an offset crossroads where you turn R at the old-style telephone box to ride NE for 1.35 km (0.84 mile) to Lowerbog road end. Initially, slightly uphill, the road soon levels out.

Straight on with the single-track road past Lowerbog road end, then at the very next farm, Auchvaich, the road starts to lose height, the downhill becoming more pronounced the farther you go. The next 3.93 km (2.44 miles) past Wester Clunes, Crochanord and Muirton of Clunes pass all too quickly and you find yourself back at the fork in no time. You could always go round again.

From Lowerbog in The Aird, west of Inverness. To the north, Ben Wyvis
lies in the background under the first snows of the year

134

STRATHCARRON, Easter Ross

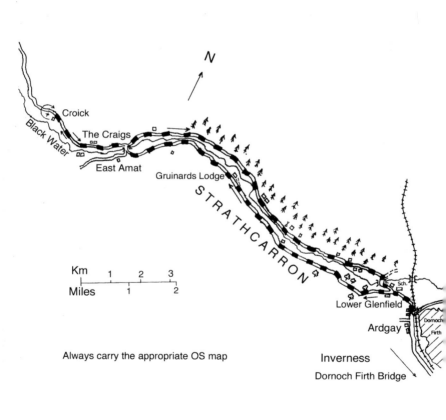

Always carry the appropriate OS map

30: STRATHCARRON

Location/Start & Finish: Strathcarron, Easter Ross, at the very head of the Dornoch Firth. Start at Ardgay, map reference NH 599 904. If in doubt, ask at the filling station on A836 (ex A9) or the café near the general store.

Route: 29.5 km (18.3 miles) all tarmac, minor roads. As much a pilgrimage to Croick Church, where evicted families scratched their names on the windows in 1845, as a beautiful tour of Strathcarron. The outward route follows the S side of the River Carron, returning along the opposite bank.

Maps: Landrangers 20 Beinn Dearg and 21 Dornoch, Alness & Invergordon.

Grading: Moderate 7. Surface 1, ascent 3, general conditions 1, length 2.

Approaches: The ride starts on the A836 (ex A9) 18.8 km (11.7 miles) W of Dornoch Firth Bridge, 58 km (36 miles) from Inverness. There is a railway station at Ardgay.

Facilities: Ardgay has a café, filling station and general store. Bonar Bridge, at the opposite side of the Firth has similar facilities. There is nothing on the ride route. Go self sufficient.

Route description: Depart NNW from Ardgay on the minor road SP Croick, initially following the railway line, then swinging W past the school. After 1.30 km (0.81 mile) in Lower Glenfield, go straight on into the road with the letterbox when the main road swings R. No SP for us. Head roughly W for 7.20 km (4.47 miles) along the S side of

Strathcarron to Gruinards. General situation is natural woodland on the R, moorland on the L.

Go straight on at Gruinards Lodge, the one with the brown gates and cattle grid, into wilder country, eventually swinging R down over the bridge after 4.49 km (2.79 miles) to a T-junction. Here turn L onto a narrow, single-track road on the N side of the river which now becomes the Black Water.

Follow this narrow, undulating road WSW past The Craigs, then WNW into yet wilder country for a total of 3.46 km (2.15 miles) to Croick Church. Information boards tell the tale of the evictions. Most etchings are on the windows at the E end of the church, where there is a wooden viewing platform.

The return route retraces the to the bridge near East Amat, then continues straight on along the north side of the strath for 13.6 km (8.11 miles) to Ardgay. When you reach Cornhill, the main road, SP Ardgay, automatically carries you across the bridge and back past the school into the village.